The best of Lakeland

Borrowdale and Derwentwater: the
Queen of Lakes, looking towards a King
of the Valleys

The best of Lakeland

HUNTER DAVIES

First published in Great Britain 2002 by
Dalesman Publishing Company Limited
Stable Courtyard
Broughton Hall
Skipton
North Yorkshire BD23 3AZ
www.dalesman.co.uk

A British Cataloguing in Publication record is available for this book

ISBN 185568 201 X

Designed by Jonathan Newdick
Colour Origination by Grasmere Digital Imaging Limited
Printed by Oriental Press, Dubai

PUBLISHER'S NOTE

The walk information given in this book has been provided in good faith and is intended
only as a general guide. Whilst all reasonable efforts have been made to ensure that details
were correct at the time of publication, the author and Dalesman Publishing Company
Ltd cannot accept any responsibility for inaccuracies. It is the responsibility of individuals
undertaking outdoor activities to approach the activity with caution and, especially if
inexperienced, to do so under appropriate supervision. They should also carry the appropriate equipment and maps, be properly clothed and have adequate footwear. The sport
described in this book is strenuous and individuals should ensure that they are suitably fit
before embarking upon it.

CONTENTS

Haweswater: now mainly a reservoir, but look carefully and you may see signs of the sunken village

The Lake District is quite small really. Just a patch, just a brownish blob on the map, with a few bits of water, a few hilly bits, a few settlements, none of them on the scale of the monster hilly bits in the Himalayas or the massive watery bits in Africa or North America. From afar, trying to find it on the map, pondering on what might be there, strangers must wonder what all the fuss is about.

It's in England, up in the far North West corner, in the middle of the County of Cumbria, about 260 miles from London, rather tucked away, not all that easy to get to. If you were travelling up from London, going North to Scotland on the M6, you would pass it on your left hand side – and if you didn't know, were not concentrating, were going a bit too fast, which would be inadvisable as the Cumbrian cops are very sharp, you could be past the Lake District in half an hour without ever realising it was there. And what a shame that would be.

It covers 880 square miles, which makes it sound a lot, as anything squared turns bigger than it is, but it's roughly only thirty miles across. A fairly reasonable, healthy walker could walk the length or the breadth of it in a day. There are only four hilly bits higher than 3,000 feet, and only one lake which reaches ten miles long, so no problems there, not on paper. Even when you've got yourself to Lakeland, opened out the map, you might well think hmm, I'll knock off Lakeland in a day, which will leave me two days for Belgium then I can polish off France in a long weekend.

If it's so small, so titchy, why have all these hundreds of books been written about it over the last 200 years? Make that thousands. In my own library, and I collect any stuff on Lakeland, however trivial, however faded, however ill written, I have over 1,000 old books on the Lake District. I'm also a judge of the annual Lake District Book of the Year competition. Each year we have at least 50 new books to consider. New books, not old ones, not reissues. They come forth in a never ending flow. I can't think of any comparable region of the globe which has only 40,000 people living there about which more books have been written. And painted. While guidebooks have been guiding us, poets waxing poetically, photographers endlessly snapping away, artists have also been artistically capturing Lakeland for over 200 years.

Then of course we have the 14 million ordinary folks who come to Lakeland every year. People, in their lifetimes, long to pack up and move here, achieve their fantasy, settle in the place they consider the most perfect plot they have ever seen. People on their death have their ashes scattered in Lakeland, where their hearts have always been. So what is the big attraction? How do you explain the Lake District's continual pulling power?

The simple answer in a nutshell, as Squirrel Nutkin might say, is in the variety. In that small space, on that small scale, you have all of nature's wonders. God's gifts to us have been encompassed in one miniature kingdom.

In the Himalayas or Africa or North America it can take forever to get a glimpse of one of the natural wonders. In Lakeland, they might be smaller, but you can move so easily amongst them, going in an hour from lush pastures, quiet valleys, gentle waters up to wild fells, tumbling waterfalls, frightening crags till you reach dramatic snow clad mountains.

The underlying rock formations change, almost every few miles, making it a perfect, compact case study for the geological history of the globe. The result is an enormous variety of colour and texture, flora and fauna, lushness and barrenness. All the beauties are manageable, get-at-able, you can take most in with your bare eyes. In some parts of the world, the natural wonders are so awesome, so enormous, even when you get there, it is hard to comprehend them. Human minds, human eyes, are too small, too limited. In Lakeland, nothing is too overwhelming, nothing is impossible to enjoy, to appreciate. On the other hand, enough people fall into those patches of water, tumble off the rocks, collapse on the heights and lose their lives each year to prove that Lakeland is not as cuddly, not as easy on the eye and foot and imagination as it might at first appear.

Wordsworth, who else, was one of the first to spot and identify this element of variety in Lakeland which makes it so unusual. In his Guide to the Lakes he wrote: "I do not know any tract of country in which, in so narrow a compass, may be found an equal variety in the influences of light and shadow upon the sublime and beautiful features."

Along with the variety of the natural beauties sit the wonders of man, from twee cottages, sturdy farmhouses to lakeside baronial mansions, historic stately homes, romantic castles. There are also museums, galleries, exhibitions, lake steamers, sports and shows, hotels, restaurants, tourist attractions of all descriptions. Well, almost. We haven't got lap dancing yet in Grasmere nor a lift to take you up Skiddaw. Lakeland is still in the best of possible taste.

It became a National Park in 1951 and is the biggest in England and Wales. National Park persons make sure that nothing nasty happens, either to the man-made features or the natural wonders. But things don't stand still. By preserving Lakeland, caring for it, the National Park has not been turned into a museum. Much of the landscape which we see today has been created by man, the surface of the fells, the shape of many of the lakes, the forests, paths, fields and walls, as well as the obvious constructions like roads and buildings. Man is now doing his best to care for them, for future generations. Lakeland has not been ruined, whatever people say, and Wordsworth was one of the first to say it, moaning on about the great unwashed coming from Lancashire or Manchester magnates building grandiose whitewashed holiday homes, thus spoiling his views and his sensibilities, or so he feared. Lakeland has

Herdwick sheep: Beatrix Potter's favourite breed

Ullswater: could this be the fairest of them all?...

THE BEST OF LAKELAND

changed, but not for the worse, not in my opinion. It belongs to us all, is our heritage. And I want more and more people to be able to come and enjoy it, as long as they don't leave litter or frighten the cows or the Herdwicks. They've had enough to put up with in the last couple of years.

There are those who want visitors reduced, a drawbridge pulled up to keep people out, once they themselves are in of course, pointing to the traffic jams in the middle of Kendal, mile long queues of crawling cars on the A591 at Rydal, people six abreast on the pavements in Bowness displaying their knobbly knees, bare bellies and orange Kagouls. They shudder, say all is lost, the wonder that was has gone. And yet you can still leave the madding throng completely, be alone and see no one, in just half an hour, by walking up a valley or up the fells or even just up a path from any settlement. I guarantee it.

The third big attraction of Lakeland – after the variety of its natural beauties, and its continuing preservation – is access. You are free to roam everywhere. No mountain is private. No fell has security gates. No entry charges on the paths. Once you are above the field line, it's all yours. This right has had to be fought for over the centuries, in Lakeland and elsewhere, but in Lakeland, it is complete. Access is everywhere.

Many years ago, we had a weekend holiday home in rural Oxfordshire, fairly handy to get to from London. It was in a pretty village, with some nice hills, nice views, but we soon discovered there was hardly anywhere to walk, so few traffic-free paths available. When we got to know the local farmers, they would allow us on some of their fields, but mostly we ended up walking on roads. There were views to look at, but not get at. In Lakeland, this privilege, this pleasure, of being able to walk anywhere and everywhere, able to spot a hidden tarn, a glimpse of a secret valley, the sparkle of a passing waterfall, the sudden flash of blue bells, and then be able to walk to it, unhindered, that is a constant joy for which I am always grateful during every day I am in Lakeland.

Blencathra: also known as Saddleback –
well known for its Sharp Edge, one of
the best ridge walks in Lakeland

I look upon Lakeland as my own home ground, in every sense of the
word. I was brought up in Carlisle where I lived till I was eighteen. We
now spend half of every year in Loweswater. In the old days, when our
children were young, we usually went abroad for our summer holidays
to Portugal. I longed for them to grow up so that we would never again
have to go abroad in the school summer holidays. Oh the hell of Gatwick
in August. Once up in Loweswater, we now never leave, never go anywhere else. And why should we want to, why go to Portugal, Spain,
France or Italy. Cumbria, after all, is Umbria with a C. That's not just a
joke, which I've been saving up for years, it's true. Umbria has hills and
lakes, very pretty, very nice, but Umbria is landlocked. In Cumbria, we
have the sea as well.

When I talk and boast and go on about the Lake District, I also
include most of Cumbria, which most people do. It does spill over, the
loveliness is not restricted to the artificial lines drawn on the map by the
National Park. It is purely arbitrary, for example, that Cockermouth is
not in the National Park, that the boundary for no apparent reason takes
a diversion, or that Kendal, the southern gateway to the Lakes, and the
HQ of the National Park authority, is not in the National Park either. I
consider the Lake District as stretching down to Furness, to Morecambe
Bay, though not perhaps including Barrow, and extending West along
the coast, taking in Whitehaven, though not perhaps Workington, and
in the North and East my Lake District includes Penrith and even the
Eden Valley, though it does not, alas, take in Carlisle, our metropolis. In
my mind, therefore, the Lake District is much, much bigger than its
political and geographical boundaries. In my mind, and in this book, the
Lake District is very much a state of mind.

So why don't we spend the whole year here ? Well, there is work in

Ullswater: note its eel-like meanderings, saving up its views to surprise you round the next bend

London, people and publishers to meet, places we want to go to, things to do, from Premiership football for me to the West End theatres and galleries for my dear wife. Two of our three children live in London, so that is another pull, another reason for not cutting completely free from London. The third lives in Botswana. Very flat, Botswana, very dry, very arid. When our son-in-law first visited us in Lakeland, he was amazed by the drystone walls. Not just by the stone itself, having been brought up in a stoneless area, near the Kalahari desert, but also by how the stone walls had been created, without an ounce of mortar. He taught himself how to build a drystone wall, a skill which doesn't have much of an outlet in Botswana, but is brilliantly useful every time he comes to Loweswater, repairing walls in our field, erecting drystone seats and hides.

Every winter we leave the fields and fells and go back to London, stoke up on urban excitements. London is very stimulating, if not exactly soothing. It's scruffy and filthy and noisy and dirty, the traffic is hellish, everything takes for ever, service is brutal and nasty, no one has time for courtesies or politeness. Every spring, I long for Lakeland, for the lake and the open fells and also for Cockermouth, for civilised shopping, for a civilised swim as opposed to the squalor of our local London pool, for a quiet meal, time to stand and talk to the locals. Every year, I so look forward to leaving London. Yet I don't really see it as a competition, London versus the Lake District. I like to think we are abstracting the best of both worlds. I like to think that what I am doing is living twice.

I boasted, back there, or implied, that I'm a real Cumbrian, but it's not true, I just gave that impression, was economical with the actuality. My love affair with Lakeland stretches back six decades, but I can't hide the fact that I was born in Scotland. Nothing to be ashamed of, though my father-in-law never let me forget my Scottish birth every time I tried to masquerade or allowed people to think I was the real thing, a native Cumbrian.

We came over the Border when I was aged four. Originally, I suppose,

Wastwater: the deepest, most dramatic, most isolated of the Lakes

from my surname, we were Welsh, about 200 years ago. The myth in the family is that a Welsh soldier at Waterloo changed sides, not joining the enemy but leaving a Welsh regiment and becoming some sort of retainer to the Duke of Argyle, returning with him and settling in Scotland. My Christian name reflects the fact that we have been Scottish since then, but I like to think I am in fact a Celt – like many Cumbrians. After the arrival of the Romans, the Celts clung on in Central Lakeland, as they also did in Wales. They each called themselves Cymry or Cymri, hence Cumbria. There are many place names in Cumbria which sound Welsh, such as those beginning with pen, meaning head or hill, as in Penrith or Penruddock. Helvellyn, that does sound Welsh, but the experts have failed to agree on its derivation.

In the Fifties, when I was at Carlisle Grammar School, I met a girl from the Carlisle and County High School for Girls, Margaret Forster, a real swot, an academic star at school, so why was she going out with me, everyone wondered.

Like me, she lived on a Carlisle council estate, so that was reassuring, but unlike me, she was and is a real Cumbrian. The Forsters are of course true Cumbrians. Just look in the local telephone directory and you'll see how many there are. They even appear in Walter Scott's poem Young Lochinvar. "The Forsters, the Fenwicks, they rode and they ran." (I've read the whole of that poem, and there's not a mention of Braggs anywhere.)

Margaret knew Lakeland well. Her Dad had taken her there on the bus, on Mystery Tours or on her bike from about the age of four. She'd

climbed everything, walked everywhere, as long as it was reachable in a day from Carlisle. I didn't know any of it. My mother had enough trouble getting herself from St Ann's Hill to the Town Hall without getting lost, never mind venturing outside the City boundaries.

So when we started courting in the late '50s, we went for weekends youth hostelling in Lakeland. She was always big and strong. I was always thin and weedy. So she carried our joint rucksack, except when we walked past houses or farms, then I would carry it, not wanting to appear a total drip.

We had a terrible row one evening at Grasmere Youth Hostel. She said we had five shillings left, from our joint wealth. It was enough for one more night for the two of us in the hostel, but we would not be able to afford anything to eat. On the other hand, so she said, we could have a meal, then go straight home. Which did I prefer?

Naturally, I chose the latter. She was furious. Took it as a personal insult. It showed I cared more about stuffing my stomach than having another night in Lakeland in her company.

After Durham University, I moved to London and became a journalist on *The Sunday Times*, coming home to Carlisle on holidays, to see our respective and respected folks. In the summer of 1964, I drove up to Carlisle in my new car. The journey took about ten hours in those days, on the old A1, through Baldcock, Grantham, Doncaster, Scotch Corner and across to Penrith, pedalling most of the way, or so it seemed from the speed. I was in a brand new Mini, price £500, and from Carlisle we took the family on various runs, down the Solway coast, round the Lake District. In each place, we got pointed at in the street. No one had seen a Mini before.

On these trips home from London, to see the family, wanting to treat them, there was nowhere to go. Meals out in Carlisle and in Lakeland were appalling. In Carlisle, it meant going to a hotel, in dining rooms smelling of stale cabbage where ancient waiters in stained evening jackets would refuse to serve you lunch if it was a minute after half past one.

Today, Cumbria is filled with gastronomic excitements. I now do all my guzzling in Cumbria, not London. This is one of the biggest changes in Lakeland in 50 years. The best known hotel is still probably Sharrow Bay, whose guests have ranged from John Major to Paul McCartney. It is now over 50 years old, the first of England's so called Country House Hotels. It has recently lost its two founders, Francis Coulson and Brian Sack, but the atmosphere and ambience, and the quality, continue. The other well known hotel is Miller Howe, created by John Tovey, now in the excellent hands of Charles Garside, an ex Fleet Street editor.

Each of these hotels has a stunning location – Sharrow Bay on Ullswater

Sharrow Bay Hotel, Ullswater, opposite, and Miller Howe on Windermere, above: still our best two hotels in Lakeland

Packhorse bridge: Mosedale Beck,
Wasdale

and Miller Howe on Windermere. The views alone make them worth visiting. But all over Lakeland there are other excellent hotels and restaurants, some with equally fine situations. My local favourite eating place at present, as I write, which is always a hostage to fortune as places will close or change hands the moment you mention them, is Zest in Whitehaven. This hasn't got a view, in fact it's on a rather nasty road and the outside of the building is pretty horrid, but we do love the food, staff and service. Back in the 1960s, I couldn't possibly have imagined myself ever saying that – recommending anywhere to eat on the industrial West Coast of Cumberland.

Looking back over my love for Lakeland, one of the highlights for me in the Seventies was getting to meet Alfred Wainwright, author of the seven wonderful Pictorial Guides to the Lakeland Fells. He drew them and wrote them, publishing them on his own at first, without an ounce or inch of printer's type, producing books which are not just useful and amusing and informative but works of art. Every Lakeland lover should have them in his or her pocket or on their shelves.

He had never given interviews, didn't do public appearances, wouldn't even let his face or biog appear on his books. Most people imagined he must be dead. When I read my first Wainwright, *The Northern Fells*, I thought he might be Victorian.

I talked him into seeing me for a book I was doing, *A Walk Around the Lakes*, on condition I didn't use anything about him in a newspaper. I saw him at his house in Kendal – a very modern, rather brutal house, which was a surprise. I'd expected an old farmhouse or twee cottage.

During the four hours I was with him, the phone rang constantly. He never answered or even seemed aware of it. Once he got going, he wasn't at all gruff or surly. He seemed to enjoy talking about himself and his life.

I congratulated him on the success of his Pennine Way guide which had reached the 100,000 mark in just ten years, with no publicity, no signing sessions, eat your heart out Jilly Cooper. It started him moaning about the price of beer. At the end of that book, he had rashly promised everyone who finished the walk a free beer at the Border Hotel. Beer had been 1/6 a pint when he'd made that promise. Now it was four shillings. That day the publican of the Border Hotel had sent him a bill for £400. He had made a lot from the book, so I did wonder why he appeared to be complaining.

His wife Betty came home as I was leaving. She'd been to Abbot Hall to hang some of his drawings for an exhibition. I went back with her and bought three of them – priced £10 each.

I started to write the cheque to A. Wai… and she said no, no, make it out to Animal Rescue Cumbria. That was the first I, or probably anyone else outside his family circle, learned that he was giving all his money from his books away to animals.

In the Seventies, we moved on from our weekend place in Oxfordshire to a holiday cottage at Caldbeck, returning to our roots. Too far of course for weekends, but we used it for half-term hols. We loved it dearly, but didn't love trailing up there six times a year or so with our three children. It was also small and dark, not much space to do any writing in.

But from it, we climbed every fell in the Northern Fells, and beyond, filling in a massive wall chart by the side of the log fire which recorded exactly who had climbed what and when. We all did Scafell in a blizzard, got there covered in snow, but goodness, weren't we pleased with ourselves.

When they were very young, it did mean a lot of bribes, a lot of Kendal Mint Cake when the going got tough or boring, and a lot of games. Countries, beginning with A, then B and C. Then towns, football teams, girls' names. Or Observation Quizzes. That family we passed further down the valley, what colour hat was the child wearing? Some of these games and distractions kept them quiet for often minutes on end.

We promised ourselves that when the children got to college age, we two could indulge ourselves and live in Lakeland at least half the year. But of course we would need to find a bigger place. We wanted it beside a lake if possible, which the Caldbeck Fells, attractive though they are, don't have. Something in a pretty, yummy, picture-book part of Lakeland, but naturally not somewhere which could get overrun by tourists, unwashed or not. After two years of looking, we eventually saw what looked like our heart's desire at Loweswater.

I remember going to the auction for it in 1987, at the Globe Inn in Cockermouth, and nearly didn't wait. The auctioneer began his spiel by saying that he considered 'it had the finest situation in all Lakeland'. Oh, no, I thought. That will put the price up. No point in bidding now. But we got it, hurrah. And have been there ever since.

In 1984, while still at Caldbeck, I began my own little publishing firm, Forster Davies, a joke name in a way, as it's just me. It publishes,

High Crag, opposite: cold cures for all urban ills

MY LAKELAND

every few years or so, *The Good Guide to the Lakes*. Surely you've got a copy. It's just a little book, to slip in the pocket, with no photographs. This book, which you now have in your fair hands, is at long last an illustrated version of what I was trying to do, all those years ago, hoping to pass on my love for Lakeland.

I have done many other books with Lakeland connections, including biographies of Wordsworth, Beatrix Potter and Wainwright. The latest one was about Eddie Stobart. No need to explain who he is, if you have ever driven on the M6 or any motorway, taking care not to speed of course. Eddie Stobart has a fan club of 25,000 members, yet he is not a footballer or pop star, nor does he appear on TV or radio. In fact very few people know much about Edward Stobart personally. He is a genuine Cumbrian, born and bred in Hesket Newmarket, and his home and HQ is still in Carlisle. Eddie Stobart Ltd. employs 2,600 staff, many of them Cumbrians. Since the death of Wainwright, I look upon Edward Stobart as the greatest living Cumbrian. And yes, I am counting Melvyn Bragg and Chris Bonington.

I do try to drag Cumbria into books or articles, even those not directly about Cumbria. I happen to have the honour of being one of the Ambassadors for Cumbria and we are all supposed to do our best to push the county. I have taken so much out of Lakeland that I feel a duty to try and put something back, even if it's just giving little talks to local societies, helping bodies like Cumbria Wildlife Trust, judging the Lakeland books, or opening things like a barn. It was a little sleeping barn in Loweswater and I was invited to officially declare it open. There must have been at least six people at the rather touching ceremony.

Of all our summers at Loweswater, it will be hard to ever forget the summer of 1995 and that amazing heatwave. I'm always saying there is no bad weather in Lakeland, only bad clothing, and I can trot out facts to show that Carlisle is dryer than Devon. The climate, up here, is not nearly as bad as people allege. The problem is that things you want to do, views you want to savour, activities to enjoy, places to explore, are almost always enhanced when the sun is out. During that unbelievable summer, we went down to Crummock Water every day for three whole months, had a picnic lunch and then swam. It seemed to go on for ever, as if the sun would never stop shining. Each evening, we were still in the garden, sitting in the shade, until at least ten o'clock. That's another thing about Lakeland as opposed to London – it stays light much longer and you can sometimes have two days in one. Chris Bonington, who lives near Caldbeck, once told me that in the summer he can get in a day's climbing in an evening, after having done a day's work doing something else.

We have had other good summers since, but none as outstanding.

Oh I do hope that in my life to come in Loweswater we have another such summeris mirabilis.

If of course it does rain, or the weather is miserable, which it very very very rarely is, then today all Lakeland lovers are spoiled for choice. There are so many things to do, places to see, attractions to enjoy. Lakeland is not just about fells and lakes, and never was. There are little towns and villages to explore, museums and galleries, literary homes, shows and sports, oh so many things which you must see, must experience.

The main object of this book is to draw your attention, section by section, under different topics, to the best of Lakeland. Dedicated Lakers will already know about them, so to amuse or perhaps annoy them, I have ended each section, each chapter, with what I think are the top three in each division, listed in order. Ridiculous, I know. How can one mountain be better than another mountain, one lake be nicer than another, one museum be more interesting than another museum. You are not comparing like with like and it's all a matter of personal taste.

But these conclusions, these final pecking orders, are my personal tastes, my personal experiences over many years of looking and wondering, all of them based on being besotted by Lakeland, a love which I hope and trust through these pretty pages I will be able to pass on to you.

LAKES

Windermere: the biggest lake with the
most boats

There are sixteen lakes in the Lake District, so most experts agree. The other bits of water are tarns. A few tarns, despite their second division status, are in fact bigger than one of the so-called lakes, but most are small, in fact very small, and some have not even the dignity of being named. It's the Sixteen Lakes which are the glamorous attractions, the crowd pullers.

Only one of the Sixteen should technically ever have the word 'Lake' attached to it. All of them, you see, have either the word 'mere' or 'water' already in their name, so there is no need for the word 'Lake'. Except one. Which is it? Read on . . .

Windermere is not just Cumbria's, but England's largest lake – 10½ miles long and one mile wide. It is named after a Norse hero, Winand or Vinandr, and until this century it was a busy highway, probably used by the Romans for ferrying troops and then later used for transporting iron ore and charcoal and passengers. Now, for the last 80 years, the boats are purely pleasure bound – but there are still hundreds and hundreds of them. In the season, they glisten from afar like tadpoles with hardly enough water to go round, or so it often appears.

Windermere in summer is not a place for peace and quiet. It is still a beautiful lake, with well-wooded shores and some dramatic mountain views looking east and north across and up the lake, but it is essentially a playground, with more aquatic diversions than any other English lake.

To escape the crowds, yet still savour the lake, get across quickly from Bowness on the ferry and walk the western side. There is no road nor any towns or villages along the western shore. You can walk a lakeside public path, most of the way, then gaze across at the mansions, and the masses, on the other side and try to pretend you can't hear the motor boats.

The ferry is a vital link for holidaymakers and for those who live on the western shores of the lake as by road, round the lake, can put up to an hour and at least ten miles on the journey.

There has been some sort of ferry using this exact crossing for about 500 years. Wordsworth went across it as a schoolboy, on his way to Hawkshead. Today, it's a motorised service, but if you look carefully you'll see how the boat pulls itself across the lake on two chains. Very ingenious.

All the public cruisers on the lake are now under one umbrella organisation. The graceful old boats of the Windermere Iron Steamboat Company (started in 1848) have re-emerged as the uninspiringly named Windermere Lake Cruises. Still, it has made timetable linking and booking much more straightforward, and the historic boats, nicely named Swan, Teal and Tern, are still in action.

The boats provide a very regular service up and down the lake – the smaller ones calling in at the Steamboat Museum and Brockhole. A full length one-way trip takes about 1½ hours, and is a great way of getting the feel of the lake and surrounding area. They run all year, but with a reduced service in winter.

Ullswater, opposite: variety, grandeur, beauty

Ullswater has not the size or activity of Windermere but it has variety and beauty and is bordered by some of the best walks in the Lake District. The name comes from the first Lord of Ullswater, a Norse settler named L'Ulf.

At the Pooley Bridge end it is gentle, flat, nothing special, but as you work your way along its length, the landscape around becomes more picturesque and then, finally, you get the grandeur and magnificence of the southern end at Glenridding.

Ullswater is a serpentine lake, snaking its way through the landscape for seven and a half miles. It is three-quarters of a mile wide and 205 feet deep and best explored from the southern end, where it is dominated by St Sunday Crag, Place Fell, Fairfield and Helvellyn. Walk along the path on the eastern shore from Howtown to Patterdale and you'll appreciate the lake at its best. The opposite side, with the main road, is usually crowded in summer and best avoided by walkers.

During the 1960s, Ullswater was the scene of a battle between the National Park Authority and Manchester Corporation, which wanted to extract water to feed the reservoir at Haweswater. As a compromise, the pumping station was hidden completely underground at the northern end and now the average visitor is not even aware of its existence.

Ullswater is a public highway and was once used for transporting

LAKES AND TARNS

miners and ore from Glenridding. At the lake foot is a hill called Dunmallet, once the site of an Iron Age fortification.

Anyone can launch a boat on the lake, either sail or motorised, and there is no registration scheme like Windermere although there is a 10mph speed restriction. Two 'steamers' run up and down the lake and resemble the cruisers on Windermere (and like them, 'steamer' is a courtesy title since they all run on diesel). These are run by the delightfully named Ullswater Navigation and Transit Company Limited and both are over a hundred years old. 'Lady of the Lake' was first launched in 1877 and 'Raven' twelve years later. They run from the pier at Glenridding to Pooley Bridge, stopping off at Howtown.

As on Windermere, the Ullswater steamers now run all the year round, though not as frequently in winter. It's a sign of the times, and a very good one. In the last twenty years, there has been a significant increase in Lakeland's off-season tourism. Cultural places as well as lake steamers now offer winter programmes. Lakeland is pretty in frost and snow and our hotels do have central heating. People generally have been taking more holidays. The result is that twice as many people now go to Lakeland between January and March compared with twenty years ago, from 9 per cent up to 18 per cent out of the total of 14 million. Think about it.

If you travel along the busy road on the western shore, *Coniston* can be a little disappointing. You can see the lake, but it is against a background of low fells and forest plantations. This is also the most 'touristy' route, with ice cream vans in every lay-by. It is quieter and more satisfying along the narrow road on the east and from here you can see Coniston Water at its best, with the Old Man and its neighbours rearing up magnificently in the background. (This can often happen with the lakes – you get there, wonder what all the fuss is about, trundle about a bit – then suddenly it hits you.)

The lake is 5¼ miles long, half-a-mile wide and 184 feet deep. It has three small islands, all owned by the National Trust. Peel Island featured in Arthur Ransome's *Swallows and Amazons* as Wild Cat Island. On some very old maps, Coniston appears as Thurston's Mere. It has been a public highway for centuries. Ore mined at the head of the lake used to be carried down to the foot and then transported to the quay at Greenodd (yes, that jumble of roads and bypasses – which cunningly conceals one or two nice houses – was once a busy port).

The lake is famous as the scene of Donald Campbell's attempts at the world water speed record. He was killed on the lake in 1967 trying to break his own record, set in 1964, of 276.33mph. There is a memorial in the village. Photographs and memorabilia of his attempts can be seen in the Ruskin Museum, Coniston, and at the Lakeland Motor Museum at Holker Hall.

Coniston has lake transport services, but it seems a shame to classify it mundanely as an 'amenity'. *Gondola* is one of the lake's star attractions, if not all Lakeland's.

In 1859, a steam yacht, *Gondola*, was launched from Coniston Hall by the Furness Railway Folk and ran a regular service up and down the lake for nearly 80 years. Eventually it was taken out of service, its engine sold to power a sawmill and the hull became a house boat. It was washed ashore in 1963 and lay derelict until the National Trust started taking an interest in the mid-'70s. With some daring, they decided to try to restore her. Now owned and operated by the Trust, this unique and beautiful craft has been back in service since 1980. It takes over 80 passengers, is decked out with luxurious upholstery and fittings and is the only silent method of powered transport anywhere in the Lake District. It is uncanny. Highly recommended, just for the experience. It's best to sit at the front – there can be specks of soot at the back.

Coniston: on the good ship *Gondola*

Bassenthwaite: far and near, still mysterious

Bassenthwaite Lake is the only true 'lake' in the Lake District, the only one which needs the word Lake attached. The others are already called 'meres' or 'waters'. It is one of the largest lakes but also one of the shallowest – 4 miles long, ¾ mile wide, but just 70 feet deep – and the most northerly of the lakes, with no real settlement on its shores. Apart from the hideous A66, which blasts its way up the west side, it is relatively unspoilt. As the lake is now owned by the Lake District Special Planning Board, it should stay that way. Always known as a good lake for bird life.

Towering over the lake at the Thornthwaite corner is a craggy white rock which looks down over the A66. This is known as 'The Bishop'. Legend has it that a bishop once tried to ride up the screes at this point to demonstrate his faith in God. His horse, however, must have been less pious because it fell and they were both killed. By tradition, the rock is kept whitewashed by the landlord of the nearby hotel. (Volunteers welcome.) On the day of the Silver Jubilee in 1977, the stone appeared red, white and blue – painted by hands unknown.

An excellent view of the lake and the surrounding countryside is available from Dodd, on the east side.

Bassenthwaite can look very mysterious – which is how Tennyson saw it when he stayed by its shores and his poetry was inspired by it.

Because of attempts to conserve wildlife in the area, shore access is limited and all powered craft are banned. There are no public launch sites. The only way to get on to the lake is to be a member of the RYA in order to make use of the private Bassenthwaite Sailing Club.

There is a shore path which runs the length of the west shore, though this isn't the best point from which to view the lake. The only access to the east shore is at Mirehouse, which has a wooded walk in the grounds.

Haweswater is one of the most isolated and difficult lakes to reach. From the central lakes you have to make a long detour by road and travel out towards Penrith. It is only accessible from the north-east and south-east sides and is in wild and unspoilt countryside. If you're only in the area for a short time you might not think it is worth it, but it's loved by Lakeland experts.

One long reservoir – 4 miles long, half-a-mile wide and 198 feet deep – it *used* to be only 2½ miles long and ⅜ of a mile wide and the water level was 96 feet lower. At its head stood the attractive village of Mardale, whose farms in the middle of the last century used to send 3000lb of butter a week to Manchester. There was also the Dun Bull, a renowned inn. Then, in 1940, the Manchester Water Corporation stepped in, spent £5,000,000 on building a 120 foot high dam and Haweswater became a reservoir. Mardale is now under the water. In very dry weather, when the water is low, the shoreline goes bleached and looks very strange and moon-like. In very, very dry weather, look out for signs of the sunken village.

Haweswater: where Mardale used to be

Thirlmere is another reservoir but was once two much-smaller lakes, called Leatheswater and Brackmere, with a footbridge across their narrow middle. In 1879, the area was purchased by Manchester Corporation Water Works, a dam was built at the north end and the water level raised by 54 feet. It is now called Thirlmere, which means the lake with the hollow (the hollow presumably being where the two earlier lakes joined). It is now just over 5½ miles long and half-a-mile wide. At its deepest it is 160 feet.

Thirlmere is in fact quite a pretty lake, very clear and pure and the woods along the west shore have a wild look about them, despite being conifers. It is best appreciated from the lovely little road which threads its way along the west shoreline, through the trees. From the A591, it can look rather barren, especially in midsummer when the water level drops, leaving a ragged, white scar round the 'rim' of the lake. One of the best and most peculiar viewpoints is at Hause Point, about half-way along the west road. You have to climb some metal steps and find yourself on top of a rock along with a garden seat. The view to Dunmail Raise is good although Helvellyn is uninspiring from this angle.

The lake has now been opened up to the public with access at most of the lay-bys along the west road and from the Station Coppice car park, halfway along the east side. There is a forest trail on each side of the lake. The Launchy Gill and Swirls nature trails suffered from tree felling but are now easier to negotiate. On the west side is a footpath, constructed by the British Trust for Conservation Volunteers, which leads to Raven Crag, an excellent viewpoint.

Derwentwater has often been called 'the Queen of the Lakes' and it is nicely compact and very pretty. But is it the prettiest of them all? Friar's Crag, which is along Lake Road, less than a mile from the centre of Keswick, has one of the finest views in the country, looking across the lake and down into Borrowdale.

Derwentwater is great for walking, but don't bother with the road. For a really spectacular excursion use the launch service – there are piers all round the lake and good walks are available from any of them.

The name means the 'lake of the river which abounds in oak trees'. The shores are still heavily wooded and largely in the care of the National Trust. It is 1¼ miles wide and therefore the widest of the lakes. (Most of them have a superlative of one sort, if you search hard enough.) It's three miles long but its maximum depth is only 72 feet. The average depth is 18 feet, which means that this is one of the first lakes to *freeze* over, and is famous for skating.

It has five islands including Derwent, Lord's, Rampsholme and St

Left: Thirlmere reservoir
Below: Derwentwater – another lazy day

Herbert's. Lord's Island used to be the site of the house of the Earl of Derwentwater, hence the name. St Herbert's is reputed to have once been the home of St Herbert or Hubert, a disciple of St Cuthbert. It became a place of pilgrimage and the spot where the monks and friars used to wait for the boat to take them across is now called Friar's Crag.

The fifth island is a real oddity. Marked on the maps as Floating Island, it is down in the south-west corner and only appears once every three years or so. No, it isn't a ghost – it's a mass of weeds and rotting vegetation which pops to the surface now and then, buoyed up by marsh gases. More of an event than an island.

Derwentwater is a public highway and was used for transporting charcoal, graphite and ore. Keswick's miners used to live on Derwent Island in Elizabethan times and the Island and House are open for visits in summer – contact the NT for times (and booking). The Lake has recently been granted Special Scientific Interest Status to help protect its wildlife, some of which is very rare.

The Derwentwater Launch Company operates a launch service which runs from Lake Shore, just outside Keswick. The launches are unlike those on Ullswater and Windermere, being a lot smaller and with no pretensions to being called steamers. They go clockwise, then anti-clockwise round the lake – though not the same boats at the same time – and can be noisy and uncomfortable, but what fun.

Wastwater: looking yummy

Wastwater is the deepest, most dramatic and most haunting of all the lakes. Wasdale was the original name, meaning the valley with the lake, so the 'water' part is redundant, strictly speaking, but it doesn't matter. It is well over towards the coast and the only way to it by car is over Wrynose and Hardknott, or from the West Coast. Approach through Greendale and you suddenly come within sight of a view which is in almost every book on the Lake District – the famous Wastwater screes. Nearly two thousand feet high, they plunge into the lake, presenting a sheer wall which goes down to the maximum depth of the lake, 258 feet. Although it looks vertical, it's not, as you can see if you manage the walk along the shore. There is a path along the foot of the screes, but it is exceptionally tough going. Best seen on a still, sunny day when the screes are reflected in the lake and can look frightening.

Wastwater is three miles long, a quiet, unspoilt lake, a favourite starting point for walkers and mountaineers. There is a good walk along the entire length of the west shore – the road is usually pretty quiet. At the head of the lake there is a very small village and the Wasdale Head Inn, which has good bar meals and a smart climbing shop. The hotel is famed among the mountaineering fraternity.

Wastwater screes: looking scary

Don't miss St Olaf's Church, hidden in a field behind a clump of fir trees, said to be the smallest church in England. In the little graveyard are memorials to dead climbers, killed on Scafell, Gable and in the Himalayas.

Although there are no amenities on the lake itself, the valley offers you England's deepest lake, highest mountain and smallest church. And the attractive Wasdale Head Inn was once run by Will Ritson, the biggest liar in England...

Crummock Water: reflects its Scottish name

Further north lies *Crummock Water*. The name derives from the Celtic for a crooked or bent lake, hence its Scottish sound. It is curved, 2½ miles long by ⅝ mile wide and 144 feet deep, and separated from Buttermere by a narrow, half-mile strip of land; they were probably both one lake, back in the ancient, geological past. It is bigger than Buttermere, very attractive, but nowhere near as busy. The approach from Loweswater, going along the east shore, is one of the best views in Lakeland with the lake in the foreground against Mellbreak. There is a footpath along the west shore, going from Buttermere village to Loweswater and this gives some excellent views up the valley. The lake is now owned by the National Trust who have rowing boats for hire. There is no public launch site, but small dinghies, boards and canoes can be launched from access land at various points.

Ennerdale: the only road-free lake

Like Wastwater, *Ennerdale Water* is on the western flanks of the Lake District and is one of the wildest and remotest lakes. Well known for solitude and quiet, the result being that you might meet lots of other people who've also gone there to be alone. The Forestry Commission have recently rather drawn people's attention to it by making noises about their valley forest trails. The valley is dominated by their plantations, but at least they have kept out the cars and allow free access. You can walk all around the lake, although things get a little scree-y on the southern shoreline. Park at Bowness Point, where the road ends and there's a good car park with WCs. Walk along the shore to the lake foot – a good place for picnics – then back by the other side. It is actually a reservoir, but the dam is hardly noticeable.

Esthwaite Water: conventionally pretty

Although not in a very spectacular location, *Esthwaite Water* is conventionally pretty, surrounded by low fells and minor roads. In some ways similar to Rydal or Grasmere, but without the crowds and cars. Wordsworth knew the lake well as a boy, but nowadays it can be easily missed if you're rushing up to Hawkshead. A public footpath runs from near the village to the shore and in the south-west is a good car park and access point. This gives a good view across the lake and is the only public launch point for rowing boats (the only form of craft allowed on the lake).

Now to *Buttermere*. The name is a dead giveaway and means 'the lake by the dairy pastures'. It is a perfect little lake. You can walk right round it, with only a few yards on the road, and the views are superb. The early tourists used to rave about it being 'the quintessence of natural beauty' and if you're based in the north and have time for only one low-level, easy, family walk, do this one. Park in the village, follow the footpath across farmland to the lakeshore. Go round anticlockwise and along the far shore you'll enter a short tunnel, cut through the rock. The story goes that the local landowner had it blasted through because he was annoyed at not being able to walk all round the lake. The lake is only 1¼ miles long and ⅜ wide, so the entire walk won't take you much more than two hours.

If you're feeling too lazy, you can park at the other end and look across the water to High Stile. You can also launch small boats, canoes and windsurfers from here, but you have to get permission. The lake is owned by the National Trust who have row boats for hire – ask at the farm. Buttermere village has two reasonable inns, with good beers, and a tearoom, but they can get very busy.

Probably the most forgotten of the sixteen lakes is *Loweswater*. This is a great shame as it is very pretty. Its uniqueness lies in the fact that it is the only one whose waters flow in towards the centre of the Lake District. There, that's one for the record books.

Loweswater is a nice, gentle lake, though looking east over it there are some rather grand views. There is a small car park at the southern end and from here you can follow a footpath right round the lake. If you prefer something more gentle, go into the woods along the west side, owned by the National Trust and provided with variously-placed seats. It is popular with locals as a Sunday afternoon sort of a place. The car park at the foot has room for only about 20 cars, which gives you an idea of how remote it is although you can get a good pub meal at the Kirkstile Inn.

Loweswater means 'the leafy lake', referring to the woods which flank one side. It is about 1¼ miles long, ⅜ wide and about 60 feet deep, which makes it another early lake to freeze over in winter. When doing Loweswater, make sure to take in the Lorton Valley, which has some of the most attractive, lushest scenery in the Northern Lakes, and don't forget that Crummock Water and Buttermere are round the corner. The three lakes go together, making a perfect string of pearls. With clever car parking arrangements, you could walk them all in a day, sticking each time to the road-less shores, taking in refreshments at the Loweswater and Buttermere pubs. What bliss.

Buttermere, above, and Loweswater:
two lakes on a string of pearls

Everyone likes *Grasmere*. And with all that fame and literary name, how could we begrudge its star quality. It is delightful, completely surrounded by fells, nice to look at from every angle. It has one island, centrally placed, no piers or steamers, and on the west side the fields come right down to the water's edge. The only thing which spoils it is the 'beach' at the foot of the lake, under Loughrigg Terrace, which can get quite busy in summer. The other drawbacks are the crowds in Grasmere village and the A591, which runs along the lake's east side. Lots of people stop along this road to take photographs. Don't. If you want to be different, go back and park at White Moss, then walk over the old road towards Dove Cottage. About halfway you'll see a seat in some woods on your right. A little farther along there is a gate. From this seat you get a good, if less panoramic, view of the lake with Silver How as its backdrop. When the lake is still and the sun is shining in the early morning, the island seems to be sitting on a mirror and the view is absolutely magic. Another classic view is from the top of Loughrigg Terrace, with Dunmail Raise in the background.

You can walk right round the lake, although you are on that horrid road a lot of the way. There is a nice little wood at the southern end. The island belongs to the National Trust. William and Dorothy Wordsworth used to picnic there and the stone barn was used to shelter sheep, which were taken across in flat-bottomed boats. Arguably the best place from which to see Grasmere vale is from a rowing boat in the middle of the lake and the island is great for picnics (but no camping).

Grasmere: a magical mirror

Rydal Water, a reedy little lake, is usually mentioned in the same breath as Grasmere – the advantage of both for the passing rubbernecks is that you can get a good view of them from the road as you whizz past in your car.

The river which flows out of Grasmere enters Rydal, then flows out at the foot down to Waterhead. If you are keen, you could canoe all the way from Grasmere to Lakeside, although the walk back wouldn't be much fun. It used to be called Routhermere or Rothaymere (after the river which flows 'through' it). It gets its name from Rydal village, though it isn't actually in Rydal 'dale' at all.

There's a lovely old bridge just to the south, called Pelter Bridge, where you can turn off the A591 onto the Under Loughrigg road. Park here and walk up the lane back to the lake. The view from the bench as you come into sight of the lake is a classic and especially lovely in winter. Carry on and walk right round the lake up to White Moss, then follow the road back. The 'beach' on the south shore is good for swimming. No public launching or boats allowed, although you may see the odd canoeist. Rydal isn't very large – just ¾mile long by ¼mile wide – but it can be absolutely superb first thing in the morning or in the winter when there is no one else about. In summer it gets very busy and for all its charm it is best avoided on busy days for the more remote lakes – unless you get up very early in the morning.

Elterwater is the smallest of the sixteen lakes. In fact, it sometimes gets omitted altogether and Brothers Water often gets included in the list instead. It is a peculiar little lake, with a funny shape tucked away at the foot of the Langdales – you get glimpses of it as you travel along the B5343. It is only half-a-mile long and has not got much to offer in the way of walks or boating. A footpath runs along its side up to the little village. Its chief distinction is the good view this path gives you, looking over the lake to the Langdales. Nice for a quiet stroll – that one view apart – but not really typical Lake District. The name is rather nice, though – Elter is the old Norse for 'swan', so this is – 'swan lake' – presumably because of the Whooper Swans which call in when migrating from their Siberian winter.

Rydal Water: a charming classic

TARNS

So much for the lakes. Now for their less famous, less popular little brothers, the tarns. It's impossible to tell how many there are as the smallest have no names and are therefore rather difficult to count, but the Lakeland artist, W. Heaton Cooper, named and painted or drew 103 of them in his classic study, *The Tarns of Lakeland*.

One of them (Tarn Hows) is in fact more visited than any of the lakes and two of them (Brothers Water and Devoke Water) are as large as the smaller so called lakes. One of the 'un-named' tarns has been given a name to show it hasn't got one – Innominate Tarn. That's on the top of Haystacks, one of the most beautifully situated tarns in the entire Lake District.

Tarn Hows is terribly popular. You see it on postcards all over the area. It's free and open and so impossible to count the number of visitors it attracts annually, but it has been estimated at over ¾ million.

It lies between Hawkshead and Coniston and is signposted simply as 'The Tarns'. There are two car parks, some public toilets and one of the most delightful views in Lakeland. It is a beautiful tarn, lush and very chocolate box, only ½mile long, surrounded by woods and with a path all the way round. To the west, the immense bulk of Wetherlam looms. Walk a little way and you get a good view down over Coniston Water.

It is usually referred to as a man-made tarn, but there used to be several much smaller tarns here, originally called Monk Coniston Tarns. Then, about 70 years ago, the local landowner built a dam and converted the marshy ground into one tarn, with two little islands. The present name really refers to the farm to the south-west. It has been in the hands of the National Trust since 1930 who do much to control the level of erosion, but with the number of footbridges, paths and fences springing up, it is becoming more artificial every year. Avoid it on bank holiday weekends and during the school holidays. Or go very, very early. It is really only at its best during the winter, when it can be very beautiful – and good for skating.

Tarn Hows: as seen on the chocolate box

THE BEST OF LAKELAND

Brothers Water is sometimes classed as the sixteenth lake – an idea which seems to come in and out of fashion and would mean downgrading Elterwater to a tarn. It lies just to the south of Ullswater, forming a well-known view from Kirkstone Pass. It may once have been part of Ullswater. A footpath skirts its shores on the west and the road on the east. Not really worth stopping for, not with Ullswater beckoning.

It used to be called Broadwater and is said to have got its present name when two brothers drowned in it, whilst skating, in 1785.

As large as Rydal, but still reckoned to be a tarn, *Devoke Water* is rather out of the way and in a rather austere moorland setting, due east of Ravenglass and only approachable on foot. From the central lakes it involves a long drag over Wrynose. Hardly worth going specially all that way, unless you're into Bronze Age settlements – there are about 400 ancient cairns and 'hutments' in evidence around the tarn, dating from around the time when the area was first cleared of forest. Much loved by Norman Nicholson for its desolate feeling. The name says it all, really – 'the dark one'.

Brothers Water: a tarn whose turn might come to be a lake

Below: Loughrigg Tarn

Bottom: Blea Tarn – but which? This one is in the Langdales

One of the largest and deepest tarns – over 100 feet deep – set amid splendid scenery, is *Grisedale*. It lies on the route to Dollywaggon Pike and Helvellyn, so is for dedicated fell walkers only. The pass was once a packhorse route through to Penrith. Nearby is a rock bearing an inscription to commemorate the parting of Wordsworth and his brother John, who died five years later – without William ever seeing him again – when his ship, the *Abergavenny*, sank in 1805. The inscription was put there at the insistence of the energetic Canon Rawnsley.

One of the nicest and easiest tarns to get to is *Easedale*. It has one of the best approach marches, right alongside Sour Milk Ghyll, with its beautiful tumbling waterfalls and small ponds. (Great for a hot, summer day.) The tarn lies north west of Grasmere village; just opposite the green is a road which leads to Easedale car park. The walk is up the Easedale Valley. The tarn itself has a rather sombre setting, though there are repeatedly good views back down the valley. The mass of stones on the left as you come within sight of the tarn are the remains of an old refreshment hut. A painting, showing what it was once like, is hanging in Dove Cottage – William and Dorothy Wordsworth knew and loved this little hidden tarn.

Wordsworth was perhaps not so impressed with the setting of *Loughrigg Tarn* which he described as "a margin of smooth green meadows, of rocks, and rocky woods, a few reeds here, a few waterlilies there", which just about sums it up. Nice to come across, not worth going to a lot of trouble to seek out. It lies on the west side of Loughrigg Fell, passed by the road from Grasmere over Red Bank.

Highest and most magnificently sited of all is *Red Tarn*. It lies in the depths of an immense bowl, formed by Helvellyn, Striding Edge and Swirrel Edge. Not as deep as it appears, it is only 85 feet. In the last century, a dam was built to supply the mines at Glenridding.

And finally, say that you have been to Blea Tarn and the response is likely to be: "which one?" There are three. The prettiest and most accessible is in the Langdales, between Little and Great Langdale. You can walk right round it and enjoy excellent views.

Clockwise from top left: a trio of tarns – Grisedale Tarn, Red Tarn and Easedale

HUNTER'S BEST LAKES

Now for the first of my top threes.

You might have noticed back there, taking you through the Lakes, that I didn't rave much about Crummock Water. This is because it is my local lake which I love dearly, especially the bit we like to call Our Beach, where we do our swimming. I don't want too many going there, but I have to play fair, and have to include it in my top three which are:

1 *Ullswater*. Has everything, really. Steamers, yet not as busy as Windermere. A brilliant, traffic-free walk along the Place Fell shore. Unsurpassable beauty which because of the lake's snakelike shape, always changes, always delights as you walk or sail the length of the lake.

2 *Crummock Water*. Also got a lovely shape, hiding its secrets.

3 *Derwentwater*. The one I know second best. You can use the little boats like a bus service, stopping off and on, creating your own walks and routes. I like its shape, unusual for Lakeland lakes in being squattish rather than eel-like, which seems to affect the cloud formations, giving an ever-changing sky.

Ullswater: *numero uno*

Left: Crummock Water
Below: Derwentwater
Extra points for good shapes

TOWNS

Bowness on Windermere

We don't have towns, as such, in the Lake District, not towns with factories and belching chimneys and urban sprawls. What we have are villages which have grown a bit, taken on a few airs and graces not to mention opportunities for retail therapy, facilities for bed and breakfasting and eating, which at certain times of the year expand and grow town-like, with crammed pavements, queuing cars, creating quite a bit of bustle so that you think, oh no, I thought we'd left all that behind.

There are in fact only three places in the National Park which take on town-like features and, by comparison with real towns, they are temporary tourist traps, rather than permanent urban centres. And they are all quite small, really, with only a few thousand residents.

Bowness and Windermere, population 8,500, is the largest town in the National Park. And it can certainly seem it on a bank holiday when it becomes the number one tourist attraction of the Lake District. Very convenient for day trippers as it is the only central LD town to have a railway station. It has the feeling of a seaside resort rather than an inland town, with most of the usual seaside amenities, but manages, if only just at times, to avoid the worst of seaside squalor and things like amusement arcades and tries hard to remain dignified, despite the hordes.

Technically, it is two towns, but they are virtually joined together and always considered as one. Bowness is an ancient village, right on the lakeside, centred round the 15th century St Martin's Church. (Martin was a Roman Officer who divided his cloak in half to help a beggar. Jolly kind of him.) The name Bowness comes from Bulness, meaning a promontory which looks like a bull's head, and it does, if you study the map, jutting out into the lake beside Bowness Bay.

Opposite: boats at the Ambleside end of Windermere.

Windermere was originally a little village called Birthwaite, about a mile away inland. It only became known as Windermere after the arrival of the Railway in 1848. Wordsworth, fearing that the horrid Lancashire hordes would soon be rushing round the lake to gape at him at Rydal and so ruin his tranquillity, tried to stop the railway. He predicted that the little village would be inundated by 'The Advance of the Ten Thousand'. He was right. A veritable explosion took place and Bowness and Windermere changed almost overnight. It wasn't just the hordes but the New Wealthy from Lancashire who built splendid mansions, many of them Italianate or Gothic fantasies, grand holiday homes to show off their own grandness. There still is a lot of money around Windermere, and quite a few palatial homes and private yacht harbours, but many of the bigger Victorian mansions are no longer private homes. Brockhole, the National Park Centre, used to be one, and so was Belsfield, now a hotel. Belsfield was built by H. W. Schneider, who commuted each day to his industrial empire in Barrow, going on his own launch down Windermere to Lakeside, then by a special carriage on the Furness Railway to Barrow. Ah, those were the days.

Windermere has many amenities including a steamboat museum, reptile garden, cinema and theatre; steamers on the lake; masses of hotels and boarding houses; rail and bus links; a de luxe hotel, Miller Howe, on Rayrigg Road; good food at Porthole Restaurant and a brilliant view of the Lake from Orrest Head where on a very clear day you might glimpse Morecambe Bay and Blackpool Tower. It is handy for Beatrix Potter countryside across the ferry and the National Park Centre at Brockhole. But oh, those summer crowds.

'The full perfection of *Keswick* consists of three circumstances, beauty, horror and immensity united' – that was said by a guidebook some two hundred years ago.

Also sometimes regally referred to as 'The Queen of Lakeland', Keswick has a fantastic setting, sandwiched between Derwentwater and Blencathra and Skiddaw. Although the population is only 4,700, it is now a major tourist centre, and has more bed and breakfast and guest houses per head of population than anywhere else in the country. The favourite centre for Lakeland climbers and serious fell walkers, it is always busy in the summer and only really attractive to walk round in the winter.

The oldest building is Crosthwaite Church outside the north-west corner of town. The foundations date from 1181, but most of the fabric of the building is from the 14th century and later. Inside is a memorial to Robert Southey, with an inscription written by his friend William Wordsworth. Canon Rawnsley, co-founder of the National Trust, is buried in the churchyard. Brandelhow, on Derwentwater, was the first property acquired by the Trust in 1902.

Originally a small market town, Keswick became prosperous with the arrival of the mining industry in the 16th century. Mining engineers were imported from Germany to look for copper, lead, silver and iron. They were treated with suspicion by the locals and forced to make their homes on Derwent Island, but they must have overcome the hostility as German surnames can still be found amongst the local population. The town also became famous for the blacklead mined in Borrowdale and so the Cumberland Pencil Company was born.

Southey and Coleridge lived in Keswick at Greta Hall and William

and Dorothy Wordsworth lived for a short time at Windebrowe overlooking the town before moving to Dove Cottage.

The Cockermouth-Penrith railway line, now closed, opened in 1865 and put Keswick on the tourist map. Most of the town's central buildings are Victorian. The Moot Hall, in the market square, was built in 1813. Keswick has loads of small hotels, a Leisure Pool, the Fitz Park Museum, Pencil Museum and Cars of the Stars motor museum, information centres in the Moot Hall and on Lake Road, a pretty little cinema and the excellent new Theatre by the Lake.

Ambleside, our third 'town', population 2,600, so hardly a metropolis, is more centrally situated than Bowness and is one of the major centres for the climbing and walking fraternity. Good for the general visitor with more escape routes to the surrounding fells and lakes than anywhere else in the Lake District, it gets very, very busy in the summer but, unlike some places in winter, it can still be quite lively and interesting when the winter fell-walking enthusiasts start arriving.

The name itself comes from the old Norse for riverside pastures and the town has a long history due to its position at the crossing of many old packhorse routes. The Romans had a fort at Waterhead, one mile south of the town at the head of Lake Windermere. Probably built around AD79, Galava fort protected the road which ran from Brougham over Hardknott to Ravenglass. Few stones remain, but the layout is still visible from the surrounding fells – especially Todd Crag on Loughrigg. Recent excavations have revealed more.

The town's most unusual building is the Bridge House, which stands in Rydal Road *over* Stock Beck. Local legend says that it was built by a Scotsman to avoid Land Tax, but it was actually the apple-storing house belonging to Ambleside Hall, when this part of the town was all orchard.

The oldest part of the town dates from the 15th century and is on the Kirkstone side of the river. This was once a centre for corn and bobbin mills and restored waterwheels can be seen just below the bridge on North Road.

Originally, the railway was to have come right through to Ambleside (there were plans to carry it on up to Keswick and put a tunnel through Dunmail Raise) but it was shelved and 19th century tourists had to come up from Windermere by steam launch and charabanc.

The teacher-training college in the centre of town is named after its founder Charlotte Mason, one of Ambleside's famous residents. Others included the diarist and close friend of Wordsworth, Harriet Martineau, Dr Arnold of Rugby and W. E. Forster.

Amenities are a Tourist Information Centre in Church Street, a cin-

Grasmere: ever so picturesque houses

ema, Hayes Garden Centre and the wonderful Armitt Museum. Ambleside is also well known for its waterfall and walk (much loved by the Victorians) beside Stock Ghyll, behind the Salutation Hotel. At Waterhead there is another Tourist Information Centre, plus the steamers, launches and rowing boat hire.

Grasmere is everyone's idea of a picturesque Lakeland village and now forever associated with William and Dorothy Wordsworth. It looks very pretty, especially if seen from Loughrigg Terrace, looking down over the lake with the village against the background of Helm Crag and Dunmail Raise, but the surrounding fells can give it a damp, claustrophobic air, especially in winter. The village is almost wholly orientated towards tourists with cafes and tourist shops. In winter it used to die completely, though the presence of gift shops now encourages the village to stay open out of season. In the summer, it is overrun – the sports field becomes a mass of caravans and the roads into the village become blocked with coaches disgorging hordes of Japanese in search of Dove Cottage.

The village itself is really a string of hamlets along the old packhorse route to Whitehaven. The road used to come over White Moss and past Dove Cottage, which was originally an inn. The present main road was built in the 1830s. Coming from Ambleside you encounter a rather nasty bend, just before coming into view of the lake; this is known locally as Penny Rock because blasting the rocks to put the road through added a penny to the rates. There is a corpse track over White Moss from Rydal. Coffins were once carried along here to Grasmere church. Up the hill, past Dove Cottage, there is a large, flat stone known as a coffin stone, where the bearers used to rest.

Most of the village buildings are 19th or early 20th century, though the surrounding farms are far older. Grasmere Church, dedicated to St Oswald, dates from the 13th century and is the scene of one of Lakeland's rush-bearing ceremonies. The Wordsworth family graves are in the churchyard.

Grasmere Sports Day is one of the oldest and most popular traditional events in the Lake District (probably dating back to Viking times) and involves people from all over the North.

Coniston is probably the most disappointing of the well-known Lakeland places. It has a magnificent setting but the grey, stone-built village has little character of its own and is almost wholly given over to the tourist industry. Its best feature is the way the Old Man rises dramatically behind the houses when seen from the village centre. The road from the south can be rather dreary, apart from Blawith Common. Still, it's a

Coniston: slate, stone, tourists

good centre for walkers, though climbers now seem to prefer the Langdales and Borrowdale.

Coniston grew up in the 18th century as a mining village, though copper was mined locally as far back as the Norman times. In the 16th century, Keswick's resident German miners were brought in and the ore extracted was sent up to Keswick for smelting. The area around Church Beck is still referred to as Coppermines Valley.

Coniston was once served by a railway line which came up from Furness. The closure of the line rendered the village rather inaccessible compared to the central Lakeland villages. Its most famous resident was John Ruskin and the 16th century St Andrew's church in the centre of the village contains his tomb. On the village green, just opposite the car park, a large, green-slate seat acts as the memorial to Donald Campbell.

Coniston's oldest building is Coniston Old Hall, a 15th century building once associated with the area's largest landowners, the Flemings.

In lowland countryside near the head of Esthwaite Water, *Hawkshead* is generally reckoned to be the quaintest and prettiest village in the Lake District. Consequently it gets very crowded in midsummer. Cars are banned from the village itself, which is a good idea, but gives the village something of the air of an open-air museum. It has an attractive muddle of squares and cobbled streets, overhung by timber-framed 17th century buildings. It isn't *too* difficult to imagine what it must have been like when Wordsworth went to school here.

St Michael's Church, up on the hill overlooking the village, is one of the most interesting Lakeland churches. There has been a chapel or church on this site since the 12th century but the present building dates from about the 15th. Inside are decorations and painted texts dating from around 1680.

Ann Tyson's Cottage is in the centre of the village, in Vicarage Lane. It is identified by a plaque, but when William Wordsworth lodged with her, Ann Tyson lived at Colthouse, just outside the village.

In 1548, William Sawrey, the Vicar of Urswick, stayed at what is now the Old Courthouse. Local records say that he was besieged for two days by a 'tumult of insurrection', men armed to the teeth with swords, clubs and daggers. They demanded that he should come out 'for they would have one of his arms or legs before going away'. Eventually, they were dispersed by neighbours. Why, or what it was all about, no one knows. The name of the village is Old Norse and means 'Hauk's summer pasture'.

Things to see include the Grammar School and the Beatrix Potter Gallery and there are good pubs and reasonable tea shops.

Hawkshead: a village dressed up
as a town

As Grasmere is to Wordsworth, so *Caldbeck*, in its own little way, is to John Peel, the famous huntsman and hero of the song. Set near open fells to the 'back o' Skidda', on the Northern boundary of the National Park, it has a traditional village green, duck pond, a 12th century church and an amazing river gorge called the Howk. Look out for the signs. Behind the church is St Mungo's Well. The churchyard has the bodies of two famous Lakeland characters – John Peel and Mary Robinson, the Beauty of Buttermere. Caldbeck is a real, working village, not yet overrun by tourists, and is home to Chris Bonington the mountaineer.

The above towns are all in the National Park, but there are many towns and villages on the fringes of the park which are well worth visiting for a flavour of Lakeland as well as a good, quiet escape from its more famous honeypot attractions on a busy Bank Holiday.

On the eastern fringes of the Lake District lies *Penrith* – a friendly, sand-stone-built market town. Its character is rather muted, spoilt by traffic during the week. One of its best attractions is the view from Penrith Beacon, which stands on a hill overlooking the town. It gives a superb view west across the plain to the Lakeland Fells.

The oldest and most interesting buildings are to be found around the church, most of which date from the 1700s. William and Dorothy Wordsworth went to school in Penrith, for a time, and in later life William wrote of the town's famous Beacon. This structure was once a link in a communication chain which ran the length of the country and was a useful early warning system when the Scots were on the rampage again.

Penrith Museum, Middlegate, was a school at one time, a charitable foundation for poor girls, then became the Tourist Information Centre. Since 1990, it also houses the town's local history museum, a modest collection of photos, documents, artefacts about Penrith's history, and assorted worthies as well as interesting art exhibitions upstairs. Penrith is short of museums and galleries, since the old Steam Museum packed up, which was a shame, but they have a new excitement just outside the town – across the M6 on the Keswick Road – called Rheged, named after Cumbria's Celtic kingdom.

Penrith makes a reasonable base for a Lakeland or Eden Valley holiday and is improving all the time. There's a railway station (though trains from Carlisle to Oxenholme don't always bother to stop). The castle – now in ruins – is open to the public and lies in the public park and the St Andrew's Church area is very attractive. There is a cinema (which is nothing special and lags behind those in Bowness and Ambleside), a very nice bookshop, The Bluebell, in Angel Square, an attractive new shopping area. There are also two olde worlde shops at either end of Market Square which have somehow survived for over 200 years. Graham's, the posh grocer's, is Penrith's answer to Fortnum and Mason. Very county. Arnison, the draper's, established 1740, is in a magnificent time warp. A sticker on the front door used to announce 'We stock nylons'.

Kendal is being spoilt by traffic and building societies which are springing up all over the place. The one-way system is diabolical. Take a navigator to make notes of likely parking places as you are swept past them, then aim for them on the second time around. It is a shame, because Kendal is a busy market town and lively culturally, largely thanks to the Brewery Arts Centre.

The best parts are Kirkland (right at the end of the main shopping street and often referred to as Kirkland Village), and the small lanes known as 'yards' off the main street. The town is also home to one of the best art galleries and museums in the region, Abbot Hall, along with a fascinating Arts Centre at the old Brewery in Highgate, and Oddfellows new gallery. It also has a cinema, now at Brewery Arts, and a good leisure centre. Not too brilliant an area for restaurants, however, but good for tea places.

Kendal itself has a railway station in the town, plus the main-line station at Oxenholme, hidden miles from anywhere to the east. The town is still reasonable for shopping of all kinds – including some unusual little shops tucked away from the centre.

There was once a Roman fort just south of the town, called Alauna. It suffered from the Scots (like everywhere else) but settled down a little during the 14th century and became famous for Kendal Green, a heavy cloth advertised by Shakespeare in *Henry IV*. The castle, which stands on the hill to the east of the River Kent, was built by William Rufus and once belonged to Thomas Parr. His daughter, Katherine, later achieved fame as one of the wives of Henry VIII. Today it is a ruin, but commands a fine view over the town.

Once the largest town in the old county of Westmorland, Kendal is now the administrative centre for the Lake District Special Planning Board (despite being outside the National Park).

For some reason, the National Park boundary line does a rather vicious loop around *Cockermouth*, excluding it from the Park. A pity, as it well deserves to be inside. Cockermouth is a fine little town, far easier for everyday shopping than Keswick, now that Sainsburys has arrived. Main Street, Market Place and Kirkgate are very attractive and the area around All Saints Church, beside the River Cocker, is pretty. The church too is good, although the wall-to-wall carpet looks a bit odd. Cockermouth has a nice community air about it, the worst aspect of the tourist industry being notably restrained. Perhaps there are advantages in being outside the National Park, after all.

Cockermouth's most famous building today is undoubtedly Wordsworth House, a fine, Georgian building which dominates the main street. The town's other notable building is the castle, built originally in the 13th century, though most of what remains dates from 100 years later. Much of it is in ruins, though part is still lived in, by Lady Egremont. It is rarely open to the public, but if you ask nicely, you might be let in.

Of all the towns lying just outside the Lake District, Cockermouth is probably the quietest and most interesting to escape to when the crowds of the central Lakes begin to annoy. There's no cinema or theatre (although the Kirkgate Centre has films and shows), and no rail links. Wordsworth House remains the town's main tourist attraction, but don't miss Market Place and Kirkgate. Also look forward to good teas, antiques, excellent veggie dinners at Quince and Medlar, three nice little museums (toys, crystals and printing), a good art gallery, Castlegate, plus the amazing Sheep Centre – thrill to the sight of 19 different breeds posing on the stage like Miss World entrants.

While Cockermouth and Penrith have crept into Lakeland, and been accepted as one of us, the West Coast towns have long been considered out of sight, if not off the map. Few tourists will linger long in Barrow unless visiting the Dock Museum or trying to find Furness Abbey or Piel Island, or will find much to detain them in Workington, apart from Portland Square, but hurry hurry to *Whitehaven*, before everyone else discovers it. At the moment, it's practically a tourist-free zone, thereby providing a perfect chance to mingle with ethnic Cumbrians.

In the 18th century, Whitehaven was the nation's third port, after London and Bristol, rich on coal exports and tobacco imports. The Georgian town had been laid out on a grid pattern by the Lowther family, still big in Cumbria, the first planned town in Britain. George Washington's granny lived in Whitehaven and John Paul Jones, founder of the American Navy, raided the town in 1778, the last occasion on which Britain was invaded from the sea.

Left: Whitehaven – walk to the end of the harbour, and it's straight on to America

Below: Kendal – walk round the town to see Lakeland life

Left: Cockermouth, Cumbria's most interesting small town

Below: Penrith – the castle is ruined, but the shops are not

After some dismal decades of decline in the shipping and coal industries, Whitehaven has come to life again. You can see it in the spruced up Georgian streets and squares. The Georgian bit is towards the harbour – Lowther Street, King Street, Roper Street. Pause a while to read the monster mosaic poem in the Market Place, then you can go to Michael Moon's amazing book shop and compliment him. (He wrote the verse.) The entire harbour is now a conservation area and has been excellently restored. Walk out on Sir John Rennie's West Pier, till you're almost halfway to America, touch the sandstone blocks, then look back and think of England. Don't forget St Bees just down the coast. Then visit The Beacon or Rosehill theatre.

Maryport was originally a village called Ellenfoot, till Humphrey Senhouse developed the port and called it after his wife Mary. Sweet, huh. Birthplace of Thomas Ismay, founder of the White Star Line, who built the *Titanic*, and Joseph Lister, the surgeon. Today, it's a smaller, but somehow sadder, version of Whitehaven, despite all that development in the Harbour. The new buildings are architecturally interesting, the new Marina attractive, the Flying Buzzard amusing. The Aquarium is good but few people ever seem to go there. In the town itself, don't miss the quaint little maritime museum.

Find the cobbled Fleming Square, walk on to the Senhouse Roman Museum, down the cliff and back along the promenade. You'll probably meet no one.

Ulverston is a typical, friendly, northern market town (great on Thursdays) with a market cross, a nice old cobbled street and a nearby canal. Overlooking the town is the monument to Sir John Barrow – a 90 foot high imitation of the Eddystone Lighthouse. There is a public path up Hoad Hill leading to the monument and from this vantage there are good views of the town and surrounding countryside. Ulverston is largely unspoilt, but shows signs of decay, which is a great pity. It holds the world's largest collection of Laurel and Hardy memorabilia in the Laurel and Hardy Museum.

Grange-over-Sands is Cumbria's riviera, according to the Tourist Board people, who cunningly photograph it to include Grange's solitary palm tree swaying in the breeze. It is a Victorian town, genteel and once a popular holiday resort. If the beach was better, it might have become another Blackpool. As it is, it tends to be popular mostly as a retirement town (known locally as 'the waiting room'), though the choice may seem an odd one as Grange is famous for its hills. The

Below: Maryport – new excitements in the harbour

Bottom: Ulverston – old monuments in the air

town is largely unspoilt and seems to be made entirely of grey limestone.

Behind the town, on Hampsfell, is a spectacular limestone escarpment, now protected but once quarried extensively for building houses and walls. On the escarpment is a peculiar limestone structure known as Hampsfell Hospice, built for the 'shelter and entertainment' of wanderers over the fell. The 'entertainment' largely consists of a direction indicator on the roof (there is a metal stairway leading up to it) which enables the visitor to 'sight' various features of the landscape. The view from here on a clear day is fantastic – from Blackpool Tower to Skiddaw.

The sands across to Morecambe Bay are very dangerous, although there is a route – if you know where to look for it. The official guide takes across parties. Crossing the sands on foot is one of Cumbria's most unusual, most exciting experiences.

Grange-over-Sands: one of nature's waiting rooms

HUNTER'S BEST TOWNS

I have a mental block about
Bowness and Windermere,
always ending up in the wrong
bit, and with Ambleside, I usually seem to drive right
through, so that's two of Lakeland's three main tourist towns
eliminated, leaving only one to
carry the flag for mint cake,
sheepskin and bed and breakfast.

1 *Keswick* it is then, if I have to
choose one Lakeland town. I
like the Moot Hall, the walk to
the Lake, eating at Maysons,
going to the theatre, but I
always make a point of going
nowhere near Keswick at weekends or Bank Holidays.

2 *Hawkshead*, even though it is
so bijou, like a film set, more
Southern than Northern. I like
the way it's been preserved,
traffic kept at bay. I always
enjoy visiting it – well, once
every year.

3 *Whitehaven* is not Lakeland, so
you don't have the tourist tat,
or the crowds. Every year it
seems to get better, more
attractive, more artistic.

Keswick: best Lakeland town, though perhaps not on market days

Left: Whitehaven – the harbour has it

Below: Hawkshead – the church lords it

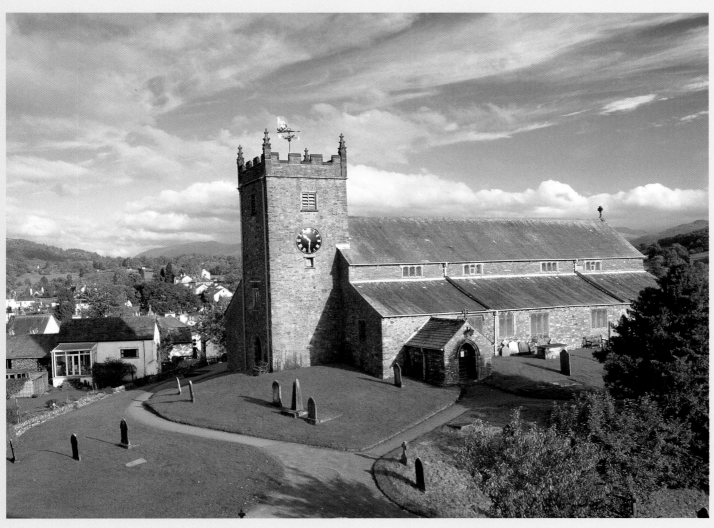

VILLAGES

In alphabetical order, eight villages worth a detour include:

Opposite: villages to wander round, lonely as a daffodil, clockwise from top left – Maulds Meaburn, Hesket Newmarket, Cartmel and Askham

The ancient and pretty village of *Askham* is just a few miles south of Penrith. Many of its houses date between 1650 and 1750 and Askham Hall is 14th century in parts and was developed on the site of a pele tower. It is now the home of the Earl of Lonsdale. Lowther Castle, which is only a facade and now mostly ruins, was not a genuine castle but a Gothic mansion built in the 19th century. Nearby is Lowther Park. The village is handy for Haweswater, Penrith, Ullswater and the Eden Valley with good pubs.

Cartmel is a lovely village, just west of Grange-over-Sands, with a beautiful square, an old village pump still standing and a nice river running through it. Very picturesque and popular on Sunday lunchtimes as it contains a number of good pubs (the King's Arms and the Cavendish Arms). It's most famous for the Priory, which dates back to 1188, though only the Priory Church and Gatehouse remains, now owned by the National Trust and usually housing exhibitions of paintings by Lakes artists. The square is often spoilt by cars – the best place to park is through the village, by the racecourse. The village is becoming a bit picture-book, but is still less of an open museum than Hawkshead.

The northern hamlet of *Hesket Newmarket*, well out of the tourist beat, was once an important market. Now it is just a pleasant village built around a long green. Dickens stayed in the village in 1857 whilst on a Lake District tour. Hesket Hall is a dull but odd building with a peculiar roof and twelve, angular projections forming the walls. The corners of these projections are supposed to make an effective sundial. The village has a good pub, with its own real ale.

Ireby Church: stuck in a field

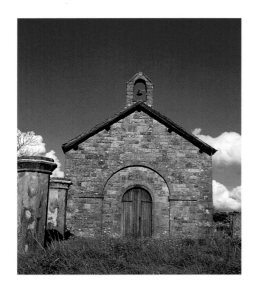

On the northern edge of the Lakes, *Ireby* gained a market charter in the 13th century but in time Wigton and Cockermouth proved too much competition for it. Look out for the original church, a simple Norman affair, stuck in a field 1½ miles outside the village on the Torpenhow road. Ireby is good as a base for the Solway Coast, Bassenthwaite and Skiddaw.

Not in the LD proper, as it's across the M6, towards Appleby, but many discriminating Cumbrians consider *Maulds Meaburn* the county's prettiest village. Fascinating stone houses, each one different, on either bank of the River Lyvennet.

The little hamlet of *Rosthwaite* in the Borrowdale Valley is useful as a base for setting off for Watendlath, Seatoller, Langstrath and Sty Head. The footpath up to Watendlath used to be quite attractive but now appears on the landscape as a mini-motorway.

One of the Lakes' most famous villages, *Troutbeck*, strung along a hillside just north of Windermere, is really a series of hamlets grouped about a series of wells. The cottages and barns date from the 17th to 19th century – the finest of all being Townend, built in 1626 and now looked after by the National Trust and open to the public. There are two old, restored inns, the sign to the Mortal Man being quite famous for its rhyme:

Troutbeck: 'tis snow that makes it look so pale

THE BEST OF LAKELAND

O mortal man that lives by bread,   *Thou silly fool that looks so pale,*
What is it makes thy nose so red?   *'Tis drinking Sally Birkett's ale.*

Note that there is another Lakeland Troutbeck, just off the A66 near Threlkeld. Even Pevsner got the two muddled.

Watendlath, a moorland hamlet of farms set artistically beside a large tarn, is situated to the east of Rosthwaite and was the remote, isolated setting for Hugh Walpole's 'Judith Paris'. Now it is a magnet for tourists and is to be avoided on summer bank holidays. It can be reached by leaving the main Borrowdale road and crossing Ashness Bridge. This road is a menace in the high season and it is better to leave the car and walk, or take advantage of the NT's free bus from Keswick.

Watendlath: moorland hamlet

HUNTER'S FAVOURITE VILLAGES

1 *Watendlath*. A hamlet, really, but so unexpected, so atmospheric, with such good walks.

2 *Cartmel*. Thinks it's really a small town, with definite pretensions, but very handsome.

3 *Hesket Newmarket*. I love walking down the main street, the only one really, gaping at all the houses, then having a real beer at the Old Crown. It's a co-op pub, with 60 co-owners, including Chris Bonington. I do like to help.

Opposite top: Hesket Newmarket —
houses to gape at

Opposite bottom: Cartmel — buildings
to admire

Left: Watendlath — scenery what won it

Opposite: Windermere Steamboat
Museum

Below: *Leccinum aurantiacum* – painted
by Beatrix Potter from a specimen found
near the Ferry Hotel, Windermere,
August 1896 and now in the care of the
Armitt Museum, Ambleside

Cumbria has so many museums, some of them quite potty and unexpected, with no apparent connection to Cumbria, such as a museum featuring cars which have appeared in a film or TV show. Many of them are the result of one person's passion or devotion. Others are traditional municipal collections. The more modern, more commercial ones are very hands-on, strong on audio-visual displays and gift shopping, but not a lot of content.

Carlisle has some fine, historic displays in historic buildings, but we are ignoring them, and the wonders of Barrow, to concentrate on those nearer the heart of Lakeland which Lake District tourists might enjoy, even on a day when it's not raining. Literary museums will be coming later. Please wait patiently.

AMBLESIDE. *The Armitt Museum* all began with three Brontë-type sisters, Marie Louisa, Annie Maria and Sophia Armitt, who devoted themselves to writing and the arts. They founded a library in 1912, subsequently supported by the great and the good of the times, such as Canon Rawnsley, Beatrix Potter, Arthur Ransome and G. M. Trevelyan. The Armitt Library now owns the largest collection of fungi watercolours by Beatrix Potter (that was an early passion, before she wrote about Peter Rabbit); early Lakeland photographs, rare books of literary and Cumbria interest, archaeological relics and literary manuscripts.

COCKERMOUTH. A small town yet with three lovely little museums. Rod Moore, ex-electronics engineer, gets upset if you call him a 'collector' of toys. He accumulated them – either to play with, or make them work. On show in his *Toy and Model Museum* are British toys from

1900 onwards, including all the famous names you've ever played with – Hornby, Meccano, Triang – 60 per cent of them to do with trains.

David Winkworth has been collecting printing presses, machines and typefaces for decades, and boasting about the museum he was going to open one day. In the end he did it, at the back of his stationery shop. You have to go through the shop to get to his *Printing Museum*, but it turns out to be surprisingly spacious and shows the history of printing from 1800 onwards with lots of good memorabilia.

Just along from Wordsworth House is the *William Creighton Mineral Museum* (part of a gift shop, so don't get confused). Its three little rooms are packed with over 200 minerals, all from the North of England, plus over 100 miner's lamps and tools. William Creighton, ex-stone carver, says his calcite lump from the Florence mine, 12 inches across, is world class. Best thing for amateurs, and all children, is to go into his fluorescent room. All the rocks light up. Wondrous.

The Castlegate House Gallery, also in Cockermouth, specialises in Cumbrian paintings by living, local artists. You don't have to buy of course, just admire the art, savour the ambience. The house itself is worth a peep, as it's one of the town's larger Georgian gems, just opposite the Castle, with a surprising garden. (Ask to see it, and the inscription over the back door. It's private, but you could be lucky.)

CONISTON. *The Ruskin Museum* has some interesting displays relating to the man and his circle, some fine mineral specimens and a collection of photographs of Campbell and *Bluebird*. A good example of an old-fashioned museum.

Stott Park Bobbin Mill: bobbin' along
since 1835

EGREMONT. *Florence Mine* is the last remaining working iron ore mine in Europe – though it only employs a handful of miners. It now also calls itself a Heritage Centre since the opening of an interesting little museum on the same site, showing the history of iron ore mining, tools, lamps, minerals, fossils, photographs, film and assorted memorabilia. How did they ever put up with the life? There are guided tours for the more energetic which go underground and last two hours. Be prepared to get your shoes red.

FINSTHWAITE. On the west side of Lake Windermere, set in wooded countryside, is the *Stott Park Bobbin Mill*. It may sound like any other little craft gallery, but is actually a major site of what used to be one of the Lake District's most important industries. It was built in 1835 and was turning out bobbins right up until 1971. After it closed down, English Heritage bought the property and reopened it as a museum in 1983. The massive mill building houses much of the original machinery, including the old water turbines and steam engines which are cranked into life several times a week. The resident curators, who are very friendly, will give guided tours and demonstrations. There are also static displays and a small exhibition and gift shop.

HOLKER. *The Lakeland Motor Museum* is a northern Beaulieu in many ways – it even has Campbell's *Bluebird*, though this one is a replica, made for a BBC television play. There are over 80 historic vehicles – cars, motorbikes, cycles, engines, as well as various motoring bits and pieces (otherwise known as 'automobilia'), such as Princess Margaret's scooter, illuminated petrol pump signs, toy cars and a walk-round 1920s garage. Fascinating stuff. They also have an East German Trabant, driven over when The Wall came down. Favourite exhibit is likely to depend on your particular mechanical bent, but their prize exhibit is the 1922 Bentley. An excellent 'fun' museum.

KENDAL. The three main museums in Kendal are now sensibly under one publicity organisation and call themselves 'The Lakeland Collections – Heritage, History and Art'. The great benefit has been big reductions on tickets for the lot, useable over a period of time, and synchronised opening hours.

The Abbot Hall Art Gallery, situated in Kirkland, at the southern end of Kendal, has one of the loveliest settings in town – right by the river and looking up towards Kendal Castle. The Gallery is in an immaculate Georgian building, set in a small park along with some of the oldest buildings in town. Just because Kendal is not a major city, don't expect another small, provincial gallery. It is generally reckoned

Left: Lakeland Motor Museum, Holker. Still bubbling along

Below: 'When I was a lad'. Figures on show at Egremont

to be the finest art gallery in the North West and one of the top 20 in the whole country.

Abbot Hall was built in 1759 for Lt Col George Wilson (at a cost of £8,000) and has been open as an art gallery since 1962. It was restored in 1992 to the decorative splendour of the 1760s. Downstairs houses a small but impressive collection of 18th and 19th century paintings, displayed along with period furniture, porcelain and glassware. It's set out in such a way that you feel as if you're wandering around someone's stately home – only without all those ropes. Upstairs the house becomes a more traditional art gallery setting to display the contemporary collection with works by Barbara Hepworth, John Piper, William Johnstone, Norman Adams and Elizabeth Frink. There are also changing exhibitions each year which are well worth looking out for.

Kendal's Museum of Lakeland Life and Industry, Abbot Hall is a separate establishment in its own right, housed in what used to be Abbot Hall's stable block. Part of the collection spills over into the adjacent 17th century grammar school, so watch out for the diversion sign as you go round the upstairs part of the museum. Small but prestigious, it won the first ever Museum of the Year Award in 1973.

Most of the exhibits are on open display – you can touch them, walk round them, peer under them, even sniff them if you want to. Some of the drawers are worth opening, too. It's a fantastic little museum, full of reconstructed workshops with genuine, hand-worn tools and instruments. There's a beautiful old 19th century printing press, made of cast iron and once used by the *Westmorland Gazette*; a hundred year-old weaving loom (sometimes used to give demonstrations by local experts); engineering and wheelwright's workshops; massive old clocks and signs; there's even a bedroom and living room, a delight to walk round, fully furnished as they might have been around 1900. One of the nicest things about it is that many of the tools and exhibits came from local people. It is all so well done that it looks as though the people who used these tools have just knocked off for lunch and might be back at any minute to carry on working. Look out for the paint shop door upstairs, covered in 'stalactites' of paint where the brushes used to be worked out.

There is a replica of Arthur Ransome's study, with many of his possessions, including his desk and chair, and the John Cunliffe Room. Who's he? He wrote *Postman Pat*, while teaching in Kendal, setting the stories in the Longsleddale Valley, with the addition of a lake, similar to Grasmere. The walls show murals from the stories, and some of the original drawings.

The Museum of Archaeology and Natural History by the railway sta-

Kendal Museum – what fun

tion, owned by the District Council but administered by Abbot Hall, is gradually changing from a typical municipal museum of the old school into an imaginative 'interpretative' centre. Don't let that put you off though... Kendal Museum was first opened in 1796 when a gentleman by the name of William Todhunter staged an exhibition of 'curiosities'. Admission was 'one shilling per person; children, workmen and servants 6d each'. The museum has three main galleries, all designed to involve rather than simply explain. The dioramas are excellent; you can wander back and forth in time in the Westmorland Gallery, go on a nature trail around Morecambe Bay in the Natural History Gallery and wonder what on earth big game were doing in the Lake District in the World Wildlife Gallery. This last gallery is fun, but doesn't have a lot to do with the area – the museum inherited a massive collection of stuffed animals and had to make a special gallery to display them in. There is a fascinating Wainwright display – telling the story of our hero.

KESWICK. *The Museum and Art Gallery* beside Fitz Park is one of Cumbria's oddest museums, more an idiosyncratic collection of strange objects than a normal little municipal museum. It holds an excellent collection of letters and documents to do with Wordsworth, Southey, Coleridge and Walpole. Look out for an original copy of *The Three Bears*. Did you know that Southey wrote it? Bet you didn't. (In his original version it's an old woman who eats their porridge – Goldilocks is a later addition.) Of the dafter exhibits, there's a box marked '500 year-old cat – lift lid carefully'; and a set of 19th century musical stones, probably the best loved item in the museum, though the literary letters are much more valuable. Each stone gives out a different note when struck, so musical visitors can play tunes – and are allowed to, but using hands only. Can be very tiring. They were played before Queen Victoria in 1848. She was not amused.

She might have been a little more impressed with the *Cars of the Stars Museum* on Standish Street run by Peter Nelson, a Keswick dentist. He has collected almost 30 vehicles which have appeared in TV and films, including Chitty Chitty Bang Bang, Lady Penelope's FAB I pink Rolls-Royce as used in *Thunderbirds*, Del Boy's Reliant, The Saint's Volvo and three James Bond cars. The 'Laurel and Hardy Model T Ford' is a genuine Ford, of the right period, and was owned by a film company, but there's little proof it was used by L and H. But all the other cars are your actual ones. An amazing and unique collection, got together in only five years. Why did no one in America think of it?

The Cumberland Pencil Museum in the north-west part of Keswick is fantastic if you happen to be a pencil freak. It has been billed as 'the story of the pencil brought to life' and lately 'home of the world's 1st pencils'. (You could also call it a museum to industrial inertia, since the graphite for the pencil works now comes from abroad.) They have pencil-making machines, a video display about pencils, a drawing competition, and a shop. (Where you can buy, wait for it . . . pencils.) There's even a replica of a graphite mine, so you can see where the stuff comes from. Don't miss the very clever Wartime Pencils – with a secret compartment, containing a compass and a map of Germany. The museum also boasts the World's Longest Pencil – 25 feet, 11½ inches long. Nowadays it's a celebrity and often out and about, raising money for charity. So if you particularly want to see it, ring in advance to make sure it's in residence.

MARYPORT. The *Senhouse Roman Museum* is one of the country's oldest and most important private collections of Roman relics. It was begun in 1570 by John Senhouse, who collected bits from the old Roman

Humphrey the boar adopted by the Senhouse Roman Museum as its emblem

Fort at Maryport, then kept through twelve generations of his family and finally opened to the public in 1990 in a converted Victorian naval battery, overlooking the town. Only three rooms, but take them slowly, if you want to savour the sexual undertones, such as the Serpent Stone, probably Celtic, and what a big one, a phallus over 5 feet high, or the 'Pin Up Girl', a naked girl carved in stone to welcome soldiers going on leave. Don't miss the earthworks outside, where the old fort used to be. Or walk northwards and try to find the site of milefort 21. The whole of this coast had its own defence system, an extension of Hadrian's Wall, with Maryport as its HQ, hence the importance of this site.

The *Maritime Museum* is in Maryport itself, near the harbour, and is typical in many ways of Lakeland's small museums. It is devoted almost exclusively to the history of Maryport as a maritime centre. Small, neat and attractive, but well run on a shoestring budget using enthusiasm and invention rather than the latest wonder display techniques. A nice change from the Heritage Interpretative Visitor Centres of this world. Collections include photographs of old Maryport and of general maritime interest and there are also items relating to Fletcher Christian (remember Mutiny on the Bounty?) and to Thomas Henry Ismay, the founder of the White Star Line. Both local lads. The museum houses a small tourist information centre and shop.

Cars of the Stars: Model T

RAVENGLASS. The *Ravenglass Railway Museum* is not hard to find as it's at the Ravenglass end of the Ravenglass and Eskdale Railway. The museum tells the story of the miniature railway and its place in the valley. There are relics, models and slides – all quite interesting. The best exhibit is the Synolda engine – a twin of the original Ravenglass railway engine which was built in 1915. It was rescued from Bellvue Zoo and is smaller than the current railway engine.

ULVERSTON. Situated in a little side street, between King Street and The Ghyll, and easy to miss, as it's in a private house, is the *Laurel and Hardy Museum*. Ulverston seems an unlikely place to have 'the world's largest collection of Laurel and Hardy memorabilia', but that's because Stan Laurel was born in Ulverston. This museum was set up by L & H fanatic (and one-time Mayor of Ulverston) Bill Cubin. Lots of posters, letters, portraits and possessions. You can even see L & H films – the museum has virtually every one available and shows them continually. A definite curiosity (and not a little bonkers) but worth seeing. If you're really keen, Stan's birthplace is on the other side of town – the curator or his wife can direct you there, but all there is to see is a plaque.

WHITEHAVEN. *The Beacon* – a handsome new building, shaped like a lighthouse – enjoys a great situation and its fun-filled contents arranged on four floors cover Whitehaven's social, maritime and industrial history. Aimed at a family audience, judging by the corny cartoon cut-outs, it's not so much a museum, more an audio-visual experience. Start on the top floor – by lift or stairs – which has brilliant views, and is devoted to the weather; not exactly a subject unique to Whitehaven, but they have lots of interactive devices about wind and water and how the Met. Office works. Then you come down through the other floors, all devoted to Whitehaven's connections with America, slavery, mining, shipping, the Lowther family – mainly in tableaux form, with model figures and sound effects. A bit thin on actual contents, but great technology.

Whitehaven's newest museum, tucked away in Lowther Street, is the *Rum Story*. Surprisingly big inside, it tells the story of the town's connection to the Caribbean rum trade.

WINDERMERE. Not in Windermere itself, but a few miles out, overlooking the Lake, is *Blackwell*, one of the country's finest Arts and Crafts houses. It was built by the architect Baillie Scott in 1900 for Sir Edward Holt, a Lancashire brewery millionaire and twice Lord Mayor of Manchester, as his holiday home. The house has been recently ren-

Opposite: the Beacon at Whitehaven – lots of sound effects

ovated at a cost of £3.5 million, ever so tastefully, and is run by Abbot Hall. It stages discreet little exhibitions but the house itself is the star, notably the fireplaces, ceilings, window seats, stained glass windows, panelling – everything really, down to the door fittings.

The World of Beatrix Potter Exhibition at Crag Brow in Bowness is one of Lakeland's most popular exhibitions, packing them in every day, all round the year. The pulling power is old – Beatrix Potter's lovely books – but the staging of the tableaux is new and the 9 screen video show very state of the art. See Peter Rabbit in his radish patch, Mrs Tiggy-Winkle in her cave, Jeremy Fisher in his pond. The video intro lasts five minutes, then you walk round the tableaux, finishing with a 16 minute film of her life. Highly organised, with groups of 25 led through at a time.

Beatrix Potter's rowing boat can be found at the *Windermere Steamboat Museum*, just out of Bowness, on Rayrigg Road in its own grounds by the lake. There are 12 antique and vintage steamboats, well displayed but not always in steam. The best thing is undoubtedly the steam launch *Osprey*, which takes passengers out onto the lake. As anyone who has been on the *Gondola* will know, steamboat is the only way to travel. It only operates on fine days, running six or seven trips a day, and can only take 12 passengers. Ring in advance to check if it is running. Look out for the beautifully restored SL *Esperance* – the model for Captain Flint's houseboat in *Swallows and Amazons*, as well as 'Amazon' itself. There's also a fascinating new display of early hydroplanes and gliders.

Peter Rabbit: in his radish patch

HUNTER'S BEST MUSEUMS

I do prefer the traditional type, with original treasures you can look at and wonder over, even if they are in old-fashioned glass cases and even if some of the treasures might be pretty eccentric, not to say potty. I usually feel disappointed by the modern museums where it's all show and display, audio fun for the kiddies, but little content.

1 *Abbot Hall*, Kendal. Still the best in Lakeland for its contents, exhibitions, imagination.

2 *Blackwell*, Windermere. The building itself is the big attraction, beautifully restored, the only Baillie Scott house open to the public, anywhere.

3 *Keswick Museum*. It amuses me, because it doesn't really try to be anything other than old fashioned.

Abbot Hall, Kendal

Blackwell, Windermere

Keswick Museum

WILLIAM WORDSWORTH

Hawkshead Grammar School: where Wordsworth, below, studied

William Wordsworth gave us the Lakes and the Lakes gave us Wordsworth. No one should leave Lakeland without communing with Wordsworth, either by visiting one of his homes in person or remembering in spirit some of the things he wrote. As well as his poetry, he also wrote a Guide to the Lakes, a best seller in its time and still on sale today in a facsimile version. At the height of his literary fame, Poet Laureate and all that, a vicar is said to have asked him, "Excuse me, Mr Wordsworth, have you written anything else, apart from your Guide Book ? . . ."

It is possible today to do a tour of the Lakes, following his life biographically. There are people, such as American and Japanese scholars, who come to the Lakes for this sole reason.

Wordsworth was born in Main Street, Cockermouth in 1770, the second of five children of a lawyer who was an agent for the Lowther family. The house which went with the job, now owned by the National Trust, is still the handsomest in Cockermouth. He wrote about it in his long poem *The Prelude*, bathing naked in the local river, chasing butterflies with his beloved sister Dorothy. The house and fine garden is structurally as it was, though the furniture is not Wordsworth's.

Wordsworth's parents, on both sides, came from Penrith and he spent some time there as a young boy. His mother's parents had a draper's shop in the market square, though there is nothing of it now to be seen. His Penrith days were not happy. His mother died when he was eight and his father when he was 13. There was no money, as it turned out the Lowther family had not paid his father's wages. His guardians did not like him, considering him wild and unruly, and they separated him from his sister Dorothy. She was sent to live with relations, while William went to board at a little grammar school on the other side of the Lake District.

Nothing Wordsworthian can be seen in Penrith today, though you can climb the Beacon, a hill just outside the town, mentioned in *The Prelude*, which has good views of the Lake District. St Michael's Church, Barton, Pooley Bridge, has his grandfather's grave.

Wordsworth stayed in Hawkshead between 1779-87. You can visit Hawkshead Grammar School, no longer a school but open as a museum with the desks and books laid out, just as they were in Wordsworth's time. Wordsworth described St Michael's Church as snow white, but it has now been un-whitewashed and stands in a fine situation. Anne Tyson's Cottage, where the poet boarded with a 'dame' or landlady, who became a substitute mother, is now a private dwelling, called

Wordsworth's birthplace in Cockermouth

THE BEST OF LAKELAND

Wordsworth Lodge, but you can admire it from outside.

Dove Cottage in Grasmere is the Wordsworth shrine and the main pilgrimage centre for tourists and scholars alike. It has come to symbolise Wordsworth's philosophy of 'plain living and high thinking'. He lived longer at Rydal Mount, but by that time he was past his best as a poet. It was at Dove Cottage that his greatest works were written.

He moved in at Christmas time, 1799, with his sister Dorothy. Later he married Mary Hutchinson and three of their children were born here. He was also joined by Sarah Hutchinson, his wife's sister. Add to that a frequent flow of friends staying at this tiny, seven-roomed house and things became pretty crowded. They moved out in 1808 to a much larger house, across the valley, but still in Grasmere.

Dove Cottage is much as it was in Wordsworth's day and is lovingly cared for. The garden has been restored and even the old summer house rebuilt. Except during the height of summer, log fires are usually kept burning in the grates and visitors are offered a chatty and well-informed guided tour. Inside, most of the furniture is Wordsworth's and the general aim is to keep it the way it was when he lived there; the only jarring note are a few items which belonged to Wordsworth later in life, but Dove Cottage got them first and rivalry between the Wordsworth places can be fierce.

Next to the cottage is the excellent Wordsworth Museum. Go there first, if you can. During the summer, you have to visit the cottage early in the day as it can get very, very crowded. Wander around on your own and it's easy to imagine what it must have been like to have lived there.

The museum houses the best collection of original Wordsworth manuscripts in the entire known universe. Look out, too, for a copy of Dorothy's notebook, where she kept her famous journal. Not all the manuscripts are in William's own hand – he used to get his wife, Mary, or sister to write out his poems for him and would then go through and make corrections. It is fascinating to compare his handwriting later in life with a handwritten poem composed when he was at Hawkshead Grammar School – it got much worse. The display is brilliantly presented and it's all in chronological order, telling the poet's life story, so don't worry if your knowledge of Wordsworth is confined to a single poem about daffodils. There are many of Wordsworth's possessions on display, including a coat and waistcoat mounted on a dummy torso so that you can get an idea of his size. There are also paintings of many of his contemporaries. Each summer there is a special exhibition in the downstairs gallery.

Wordsworth had two other homes in Grasmere, neither of them

open to the public. Allan Bank, where he moved in 1808, is a large house, easily seen from down by the lake as it is above the village, directly under Helm Crag. Quite a nice old house, with magnificent views over Grasmere. It is owned by the National Trust, but rented privately. It used to be white, but was repainted buff for Ken Russell's Coleridge film.

The second house is the Old Parsonage, opposite St Oswald's Church. Wordsworth moved there in 1811, because the chimneys at Allan Bank smoked too much and he fell out with the landlord. By

1813, two of William's children had died at the Parsonage, so he and Mary decided to quit Grasmere Vale altogether and move to Rydal.

Rydal Mount, Ambleside, was William's final home until his death in 1850. In his own lifetime, it became a poetical shrine to his fans – he would sometimes receive as many as a hundred visitors a day, flocking to the gate just in the hope of a glimpse of the great man. He became Poet Laureate and would issue great pronouncements on the purpose and structure of poetry. (He has the distinction of having been a Poet Laureate who never wrote a line of official verse.) It is a somewhat grander house than their previous homes and William and Dorothy both thought they had gone up in the world. Once something of a rebel, by now William was a staunch supporter of the old order. The cuckoo clock that now hangs in Dove Cottage was once at Rydal Mount and its ticking used to soothe him to sleep. One night in 1850 it struck midnight and on the twelfth stroke, William died.

Originally a 16th century farmhouse, the house is still owned by a descendant of William's. It is set in beautiful grounds – originally landscaped by Wordsworth – and contains a lot of his furniture, manuscripts and possessions. When William died, most of his effects were sold off and bought by local people. Over the years, they have gradually been returned to their former homes.

At the bottom of the lane to Rydal Mount, just behind the church, is an area of land now owned by the National Trust and called Dora's Field. This has nothing to do with the daffodils of William's poem, as some visitors assume, but was a field given to his daughter by the poet. The real site for those notorious daffodils is on the west shore of Ullswater, in Gowbarrow Park (also owned by the National Trust and accessible). William and Dorothy passed through the park in 1802, when on their way to visit their friends, the Clarksons, at Eusemere, near Pooley Bridge.

The final pilgrimage site for all Wordsworth fans is back in Grasmere, where William, Mary and Dorothy are buried in the churchyard.

Opposite: Rydal Mount, Wordsworth's final home. The Wordsworths' graves, above, are in Grasmere

THE LAKE POETS

Wordsworth gathered about himself quite a circle of other literary notables of the period. They became known as the Lake Poets, though in style there was little connection between them.

Samuel Taylor Coleridge was the first. As soon as the Wordsworths were installed in Dove Cottage, he moved up to Greta Hall, in Keswick, just to be near them. He would often walk over to Dove Cottage for the evening, sometimes coming via Helvellyn. Coleridge was a notable walker and toured the Lakes extensively. In 1802, he made the first recorded ascent of Broad Stand on Scafell – a walk which has since become too dangerous to follow without ropes.

Robert Southey joined Coleridge at Greta Hall in 1803. They were brothers-in-law and Southey eventually ended up supporting Mrs Coleridge when her husband was pursuing Sarah Hutchinson (Wordsworth's sister-in-law) – which perhaps explains his frequent visits to Dove Cottage. Southey wrote hardly any verse directly connected with the area, but he wrote the original version of *The Three Bears*, a good piece of children's verse about the Lodore Falls and a

Poetic inspiration: daffodils, Ullswater

fine biography of Nelson. He also wrote the first official history of Brazil and the government of that country paid for the memorial to him which is now in Crosthwaite Church, Keswick. He never went to Brazil.

Southey spent almost all his adult life in the Lakes. He became Poet Laureate in 1813 and between them, Southey and Wordsworth made the Lakes the centre of English poetry for several decades. Southey died at home in Keswick in 1843 – and Wordsworth took over as Laureate.

Thomas De Quincey is now most famous for writing a book called *Confessions of an English Opium-Eater*, but he also wrote a wonderful book of gossip and memories of the Lake Poets, called simply, *Recollections of the Lakes and Lake Poets*. He was an early fan of Wordsworth – although the great man treated him rather badly later in life – and made three separate attempts to visit his hero at Dove Cottage, coming up all the way from Oxford. Each time his nerve failed him and he retreated. He finally got there in 1807 and eventually took over the lease when Wordsworth and family moved out. Dorothy made him some curtains and was amazed at the huge quantities of books he installed in the house. He upset the family almost at once by knocking down their summer house and cutting down the orchard to let more light into the cottage. Dorothy refused to speak to him after that. The Wordsworths further snubbed him when he began an affair with a local farmer's daughter, whom he eventually married. She came from Nab Cottage. It is beside the A591, looking over Rydal Water. It is not strictly open to the public, and is run by Mr and Mrs Melling as the 'Nab Cottage English Language in the Lakes Experience' (well, they do have to keep up the reputation for eccentricity . . .). They still have De Quincey's desk there. He moved into The Nab in 1829, though he kept on Dove Cottage to house all the books. In 1835 he tried to buy it for £130.

De Quincey became the second editor of *The Westmorland Gazette* but got the sack for not going to the office. A tenant of Dove Cottage for 27 years, he only lived there for 15 and died in Edinburgh in 1859.

JOHN RUSKIN

John Ruskin, art-critic, writer, philosopher and champion of many social causes, first came to the Lakes as a young boy in 1824. In 1871, at the age of 52, he decided to settle here and bought Brantwood on Coniston for £1,500, without even first seeing the place. "Any place opposite Coniston Old Man *must* be beautiful," he said. In the event, he got

Samuel Taylor Coleridge

Robert Southey

Thomas De Quincey

John Ruskin: self-portrait
Below: the gardens of his Brantwood
home

"a mere shed of rotten timbers and loose stone", but he transformed it into a beautiful home, stocked it with art treasures (particularly the paintings of Turner, of whom he was an early champion) and lived there for the last 30 years of his life. Today, Brantwood is open to the public (which was Ruskin's original wish), transformed into an excellent museum and country house. It now rivals the other Lake District big guns (Dove Cottage, Hill Top and Rydal Mount).

The house contains many of Ruskin's paintings and possessions – look out for the Ruskin-designed wallpaper in the downstairs rooms. The political message of his writings still comes across in a video of his life and work, on constant show in one of the downstairs rooms. Ruskin fought hard against the worst aspects of Victorian society and values. Sobering to realise how much of it is relevant today.

Brantwood stands in 250 acres of grounds and there's a good nature trail and a jetty to bring people across to Brantwood by the Gondola service.

The Ruskin Museum is down in Coniston village and a monument to him stands at Friar's Crag on Derwentwater, bearing the following quote: "The first thing I remember as an event in life was being taken by my nurse to the brow at Friar's Crag on Derwentwater."

BEATRIX POTTER

Beatrix Potter was a Londoner, born there in 1866, but her family had connections with Lancashire cotton and she spent her holidays from the age of 16 in the Lake District, in rented, but rather grand, houses round Windermere and Derwentwater. Her parents were genteel, upper middle class Edwardians and she was educated at home and expected to devote her life to her parents, or get married. She found an outlet for artistic talents in drawing and painting "little books for children" and encouraged by the family's Lakeland friend, Canon Rawnsley, her first book, *The Tale of Peter Rabbit*, was published in 1901.

Beatrix Potter

The money she made with her books she used to buy Hill Top Farm at Near Sawrey in 1905. Over the next eight years, she wrote another 13 children's books, mostly while she was in the Lake District. In 1913, she married William Heelis, a local solicitor, and after that devoted her life to her farms and to the preservation of the countryside, doing a great deal to help the work of the National Trust, thanks again to the friendship and encouragement of Canon Rawnsley.

Beatrix Potter died in 1943. All her property, 15 farms with their Herdwick flocks, many cottages and 4,000 acres of land, came to the National Trust. She asked that the Herdwicks, her favourite sheep, should continue to be bred, and that both farms and cottages should have local, reliable, tenants.

Beatrix Potter built an extension to Hill Top for her tenant farmer, but kept the original 17th century building for her own use. She wrote many of her books there and sometimes was able to stay for a few nights but at no time did she actually live there. Nearby Castle Cottage became her home after she married William Heelis.

Hill Top, which contains Beatrix Potter's furniture, is small and very popular, with 90,000 visitors going through it in the peak year of 1979. It is the duty of the National Trust to protect its properties, in this case against the fabric of the building being eroded by the sheer number of visitors, so restrictions have since been introduced by limiting numbers allowed into the house at any one time, making no reductions for parties, not permitting coaches and shutting the house on Thursdays and Fridays. It must be one of the very few houses open to the public where they go to such lengths to restrict the public. Best to go mornings, as once the target of 800 visitors a day is reached, you've had it.

For several years visitors to Hill Top were disappointed to find that the original watercolours from the Beatrix Potter books were not on show – till they reappeared, and in a marvellous setting at The

Beatrix Potter Gallery in Main Street, Hawkshead. The National Trust has converted the original legal offices of William Heelis, BP's husband, and turned it into an excellent little gallery. There's also a recreation of Mr Heelis's office, complete with his desk ledgers and period files.

It is nice to be able to compare the printed illustrations with the early sketches and paintings. A shame the NT has concentrated on Peter Rabbit et al., to the exclusion of Beatrix Potter's other water-colours (such as her flower paintings which are exquisite). For her other botanical watercolours visit the Armitt collection in Ambleside.

MIREHOUSE

Opposite: Mirehouse, still the home of the Speddings

The final major literary home in the Lakes which is open to the public is Mirehouse on the eastern shore of Bassenthwaite, four miles north of Keswick on the A591. It was once the home of James Spedding, a noted literary figure of the 19th century, the author of a 14-volume biography of Francis Bacon. One of his more notable visitors at Mire-house was Tennyson, who stayed there whilst working on his version of the Arthur Legend. He used Bassenthwaite in his description of Arthur's death – it was on this lake that the black barge bore away King Arthur's body in *Idylls of the King*.

Thomas Carlyle was a frequent visitor to Mirehouse. He said that it was "beautiful and so were the ways of it . . . not to speak of Skid-daw and the finest mountains on earth". Not only was James Spedding the host for some of the literary notables of his day, his family also had literary connections. His father, John, spent six years in the same class as Wordsworth at Hawkshead Grammar School. Some of Words-worth's letters – along with those of Southey and Hartley Coleridge – can be seen at Mirehouse.

Still in the Spedding family, Mirehouse today is the epitome of the English country manor house. Very often a pianist is playing. The rooms are delightful, the house historic and the setting majestic. It has a nature trail in the grounds and Bassenthwaite Lake's only east-shore walk.

The Speddings are likely to be on hand – if so, ask them to let you hear their Tennyson recording, reciting *The Charge of the Light Brigade*.

Most of the writers of the 19th century seem to have visited the Lake District and many took on holiday homes or even settled there.

Harriet Martineau built the Knoll, at Ambleside, and lived there for 30 years. She wrote *The Complete Guide to the English Lakes* (but didn't give top three ratings to anything). She was a friend of Wordsworth and her visitors included at various times Charlotte Brontë, George Eliot and Matthew Arnold.

Felicia Hemens also became a resident of Ambleside and lived at Doves Nest. Not very famous today, but she wrote *The Boy Stood on the Burning Deck* and spawned a host of parodies.

Charles Dickens and Wilkie Collins toured the area in 1857, describing their travels in *The Lazy Tour of Two Idle Apprentices*. They stayed at the Queen's Head Inn at Hesket Newmarket (now a private house) and went on an ill-advised expedition to climb Carrock Fell, getting caught in rain and mist.

Sir Hugh Walpole moved to Brackenburn in 1923, a house on the south-west shore of Derwentwater. His four famous *Herries* novels were set in Borrowdale. The home of Judith Paris can be seen at Watendlath, beside the tarn.

Arthur Ransome went to school in Windermere and the Winster Valley and lived as an adult near Coniston. He based many of his famous children's stories on local places – the Swallows and Amazons books are said to amalgamate the Lakes of Windermere and Coniston. He died in 1967 and is buried in Rusland Churchyard.

Harriet Martineau

HUNTER'S BEST LITERARY SHRINES

The top two are easy, uncontroversial, attracting visitors from all over the world. They do have such genuine atmosphere and convey a real sense of the person who was once there. Dove Cottage has to be tops as the Wordsworth Museum is nearby, making it the world HQ of the Wordsworth Industry. They hate it when you use that expression but I mean it as a compliment — they have been so industrious in promoting our William.

1 *Dove Cottage*, Grasmere

2 *Hill Top*, Sawrey

3 *Brantwood*, Coniston. Home of John Ruskin, below

Dove Cottage: winner for Wordsworth
worshippers

Hill Top: best for Beatrix Potter buffs

ACTIVITIES

Tak hod: it's Cumberland and
Westmorland wrestling

There are sports and activities which are peculiar to Cumbria, and
some are very peculiar indeed, which you will see nowhere else in the
world. The place to see them is usually at one of the Cumbrian Shows
or Sports held regularly in the same village or town, in the same show
field, on the same day of the month. Even the smallest ones normally
have a combination of Cumbrian sports with agricultural and live-
stock displays and competitions.

Cumberland and Westmorland wrestling is the most famous of the native
sports, practised at most of the main shows. It began with Norsemen
and at one time was widespread across the country. Today it is
almost exclusively Cumbrian and a feature of many of the sports and
agricultural shows. It looks like a trial of strength but is actually
quite technical. The best wrestlers usually follow in family tradition
and seem to be practically bred for it. Just like the best animals.

Two men face each other in a small arena, watched by two judges
and a referee. The wrestlers are usually dressed in costumes which
resemble combinations and embroidered bathing trunks. After shak-
ing hands, the two men 'tak hod', that is, lock arms behind each
other's back. The aim is to try to topple the other fellow to the
ground and break his hold. If both fall, the one on top is the winner.
The secret lies in tempting your opponent into a position of apparent
security and then quickly overbalancing him. To the casual spectator,
the technical subtleties are often not very obvious, but the events
usually have a sense of atmosphere and tradition which make them
well worth attending.

Another principal attraction of a Lake District sports day is *fell racing*. It consists of a race to the top of the nearest fell, often a gruelling 1,500 foot struggle, round a flag at the summit, then a breakneck dash back down into the arena. A straightforward, though torturous race. The best of all is the Grasmere guides' race (nothing to do with boy scouts and brownies) which can be quite spectacular and very exciting to watch. The Lake District is home to numerous fell races where contestants set themselves seemingly impossible tasks to achieve in as short a time as possible. One of the best known is the Bob Graham Round – 72 miles, 42 peaks – supposed to be completed in 24 hours. Only 50 per cent of challengers manage it.

Fell racing: because it's there, waiting to be run up

Nowadays, *sheep dog trials* take place all over the country and are well known to everyone through television, but they began in the north of England. The first took place in Northumberland in 1876 and the following year sheep dog trials were being held on Belle Isle, Windermere. In 1891, the 'Lake District Sheep Dog Trials Association' was formed.

Five sheep are released at one end of the arena – up to a quarter of a mile away – and the shepherd has to remain at his post whilst his dog – usually a Border Collie – gathers the sheep and brings them towards the shepherd through a series of obstacles. The final and most difficult part is to coax the sheep into a pen and it is only at this stage that the shepherd is able to assist, other than by whistling and calling.

Towards the end, the tension can build up quite rapidly and there is often a sense of magic about the way the shepherds can control their dogs. These events are very popular and set against the Lakeland fells on a fine, summer day, you are seeing them at their best. They often form a part of an agricultural or sports show but it is best to see them at the Rydal or Patterdale Sheep Dog Trials for the greatest sense of atmosphere.

Fox hunting is not unique to Lakeland, though the sport's most famous exponent – John Peel – is buried in Caldbeck churchyard. Cumbrian fox hunting on the fells is radically different from the 'polite' social occasions of the south. The Lakeland farmer hunts primarily to kill foxes and keep down their numbers – and does it on foot. The hunt followers no doubt have reasons of their own. There are no horses and red coats – all the members hunt on foot and only one, the huntsman, wears the red coat. Hunt followers can be seen parked beside the road at the foot of the fells, whence comes the disembodied baying of the hounds.

There are six main packs in Cumbria: Blencathra – reckoned to be the premier pack – established in 1840, operating in the countryside around Thirlmere, Derwentwater, Skiddaw and Caldbeck; Melbreak – the north-west fells and out to the coast; Ullswater – around Kentmere, Fairfield and out towards Penrith; Eskdale and Ennerdale – south-west Lakeland, Scafell and into Langdale and out to the coast; Coniston – the central Lakes and east of Windermere; and Lunesdale – out over the Pennines.

The fox-hunting season extends from the beginning of October through until the end of April. Neither the time nor the sport is particularly convenient for the holidaymaker to the Lakes. But should you winter in Lakeland, look out for it.

Hound trailing has been a favourite sport in Cumbria for more than a hundred years and probably originally derived from the method used by huntsmen to train foxhounds. It is really fox hunting without the fox, done in the summer off-season, so it's perfect for visitors to watch. From a starting point, a trail is set down by dragging an aniseed-soaked cloth over the fellside, making the course as difficult as possible by including fences, hedges, walls and a variety of terrain. For a fully-grown dog, the trail can be up to 10 miles long and can take 25 to 45 minutes to complete.

After the scent has been laid, the hounds are released; they pick up the scent from the 'trailer', then the whole pack rushes off into the hills. They might be out of sight until the finish, when they follow the trail back and the owners shout, whistle and wave to coax their animals over the line. The end can be quite exciting, but for most 'serious' spectators the attraction lies in betting which hound will win. The local Cumbrian bookies, who appear at most big sports, are a feature in themselves.

EVENTS

The two biggest and best known are the Grasmere Sports and the Ambleside Sports, each held every year in August. Grasmere features throwing and cycling events, attracting professionals from all over the country, along with the best of the traditional, local events, such as Cumberland and Westmorland wrestling. In addition, there is a contest for the best costume worn by the wrestlers as well as the famous guides' fell race and hound trailing.

Ambleside Sports take place in Rydal Park, just north of Ambleside. It began before the First World War, was revived again about 30 years ago and is now one of the biggest events of its kind in the Lake District, with track events, fell races and Cumberland and Westmorland wrestling, all in a lovely, fellside setting.

Other Cumbrian shows worth looking out for are the Westmorland County Show, the Ennerdale Show, Eskdale Show, Gosforth Show, Hawkshead Show, Keswick Show, Wasdale Show, Egremont Crab Fair and the Loweswater Show.

The Egremont Crab Fair, which dates back to 1267, includes the famous World Gurning championships. The entrants put their heads through a horse collar and grin or 'gurn' – the object being to pull a revolting expression; the most grotesque wins. Entrants with dentures tend to have an advantage here, though it is said that one year the contest was won by a sympathetic onlooker who was just watching.

And finally, in the World Championship stakes, is the Biggest Liar in the World competition. This eccentric little competition, administered by Copeland Borough Council, takes place every year in November at the Santon Bridge Inn. It dates back to Will Ritson, a 19th century publican who lived at the head of the Wasdale valley. 'Auld Will' was a genuine and sincere man who lied constantly; one tale was that turnips in Wasdale grew so big that the dalesfolk quarried into them for their Sunday lunch and then used them as sheds for the Herdwick sheep. The contest is held strictly for amateurs – politicians, journalists and lawyers are barred from entry. Price of admission includes an excellent tatie pot supper.

The Eskdale Show: top tup

HUNTER'S BEST ACTIVITIES

1 *Cumberland and Westmorland Wrestling*

2 *Hound Trailing*

both of them unique in their form to Cumbria

HUNTER'S BEST SHOWS

1 *Grasmere*

2 *Ambleside*

3 *Loweswater*

Fell racing at Grasmere Sports,
Wrestling at Ambleside and the
Loweswater Show

STATELY HOMES

Sizergh Castle: home to the Stricklands for 700 years

Cumbria's stately homes tend not to be in central Lakeland, for obvious reasons. Rather hard to build them on top of mountains. But it's also to do with the fact that, historically, big estates with big landed gentry tended to be created on the plains, on the lush pastures, rather than on the rough, unprofitable fells.

So Cumbria's nobs and assorted aristocracy, of which there are a great many, are thicker on the ground in the Southern Lakes or towards the East, near Penrith. Which does mean they are pretty easy to get to for Lakeland visitors.

Like stately homes everywhere, which have been thrown open to the public, many of them try to offer other attractions as well, from tearooms to motor museums and special events, hoping to attract the crowds. At a price of course. But there are other buildings and erections, such as churches and monuments, which are usually free. Often because they are stuck in the middle of a field, miles from anywhere.

Dalemain, near Penrith is fascinating architecturally. A large, Georgian-fronted building with extensive grounds, the house itself is medieval, Elizabethan and early Georgian and contains family portraits of the Hasells, who have lived there since 1665. It has a magnificent garden, famous for rare trees and shrubs, and a fantastic tea shop in a baronial hall. There's also a small museum of agricultural bits and pieces in the 16th century barn.

Holker Hall in Cark-in-Cartmel is an outstanding country house, dating back to the 17th century and now owned by the Cavendish family and set in a 120-acre park. The site itself used to belong to Cartmel Priory. It contains some beautiful examples of panelling and wood carving and some rare paintings including works by Van Dyck and Joshua Reynolds. A genuine 'stately home' but without ropes and restrictions. The gardens are wonderful and contain what is said to be the oldest monkey puzzle tree in the country. There's a lot going on at Holker, which can sometimes put you off as it sounds more like a country fair than a stately home with model aircraft rallies, hot-air ballooning and vintage car rallies. All very professionally done, but if you want to see the house and grounds at their best, go when none of these wonders are on. The gardens are best in early summer and there's a Garden Festival in May/June.

Holker Hall: seat of the Cavendish family

Situated off the B5305 between Penrith and Wigton, and originally a 14th century pele tower with 17th, 18th and 19th century additions, *Hutton-in-the-Forest* is the home of Lord and Lady Inglewood. It has a nice, amateur feel to it and you sense that the running of it isn't too severely professional. You get the distinct feeling that the occupants are around. Which they usually are. Very satisfying, architecturally, it is like visiting three stately homes in one. There are good gardens with some excellent tree specimens, open daily except Saturday, but the House has some peculiar opening days. You have to be smart to catch it open. The tea shop is very good.

Hutton-in-the-Forest: home to the Inglewoods

Five miles south of Kendal, situated by Levens Bridge, lies the magnificent Elizabethan mansion of *Levens Hall* — although it originally began as a Norman pele tower. It houses some fine paintings, furniture and plasterwork and a fascinating fireplace in the south drawing room with carvings depicting the four seasons, the four elements and the five senses. There's also a very good topiary garden laid out in 1692.

Levens Hall is trying very hard to be a stately home on the southern model, providing lots of fun for kiddies, of all ages, such as their Steam Collection (in steam on Sunday afternoons and Bank Holidays). The House is run, owned and lived in by the Bagot family. It can be a bit too commercial for some tastes, but they are trying. Look out for their special exhibition on Admiral Percy, who started as a midshipman with Nelson on HMS Victory.

There are occasional guided tours of the garden, which are worth going on, especially the water garden.

Levens Hall: tops for topiary

Although it may seem strange to feature a castle in this section, we can blame the Scots who are indirectly responsible for the architecture of many of Cumbria's historic homes. Like many others, *Muncaster Castle*, Ravenglass, is based on a defensive pele tower, built in 1325, to keep them at bay. In the 1860s, the fourth Lord Muncaster had it rebuilt to make a tasteful mansion, still lived in by the Pennington family as their ancestral home since the 13th century. Paintings include some by Reynolds and Gainsborough.

The gardens are magnificent in early summer when the rhododendrons and azaleas are at their best. Viewed against the background of the Lakeland fells, they are spectacular – one of the finest displays in Europe. Muncaster Castle is also the headquarters of the British Owl Breeding and Release Scheme.

Muncaster Castle: from pele to owls

Sizergh Castle, Kendal, has been the home of the Strickland family for 700 years. There was an original house there, but this was replaced in 1340 with a pele tower. Those Scots again. It is the largest tower in Cumbria still standing. The great hall was added in 1450 and has some very fine panelling and carving added in Elizabethan times – some of the finest in the country. A lovely house, the gardens date from the 18th century. Great on a warm, sunny day. Now owned and run by the National Trust.

Sizergh Castle: largest tower in Cumbria

Finally, in contrast to the above stately homes, *Townend* at Troutbeck, near Windermere, is a dark little place, but very typical of its period. A 1626 statesman farmer's residence – rather more prosperous than your average farmhouse – in an interesting, unspoilt hamlet. Contains some surprisingly elaborate furniture and panelling. Run by the National Trust, which has recently opened three new rooms, once used by servants, it has a small garden laid out to resemble a photograph of Townend from the late 19th century.

Townend: good state for a statesman

CHURCHES

Cumbria has a host of interesting churches although they tend not to be as ornate or rich, either outside or inside as some southern churches. Many of them, especially near the borders, were semi-fortified to repel raiders but they are all rich in history and archaelogical interest.

Cartmel Priory, Cartmel, was founded by William Marshall, the Baron of Cartmel, in the late 12th century. Nothing remains of the original priory except the gatehouse (National Trust) and church. The gatehouse is open to the public, just off Cartmel Square. The church has been restored several times and is now a collection of styles; the east window is 15th century. The best feature is the carved oak misericords, with some delightful mermaids, apes, elephants and unicorns.

Furness Abbey

Located in a small valley, midway between Barrow-in-Furness and Dalton, east of the A590, *Furness Abbey* was mentioned by Wordsworth. It is now a ruin in the care of English Heritage (the two facts are not connected). The remains are very impressive, some parts almost at their original height. It dates from around 1127 and the layout can be clearly seen – in sections. The walls rear overhead and you get the powerful feeling of the monastery's size and influence.

Conishead Priory, Ulverston, is now the home of a Buddhist monastery, lived in by about 100 members of the Manjushri Mahayana community. The 19th century Gothic priory was derelict when they took it over in 1976, it having been at various times a hotel and then a convalescent home for Durham miners, but they are carefully and slowly restoring it. It is an amazing house, one of the most spectacular in Cumbria, with turrets and spires, cloisters, massive stained glass windows, wood panelling and 70 acres of wooded ground which go down to the shore of Morecambe Bay. The Buddhists, rather friendly folks, allow you into the house and grounds at weekends all summer, and don't even charge, unless you go on a conducted tour. There's a tasteful, ever so healthy, cafe and a small souvenir shop, surprisingly strong on Buddhist gifts.

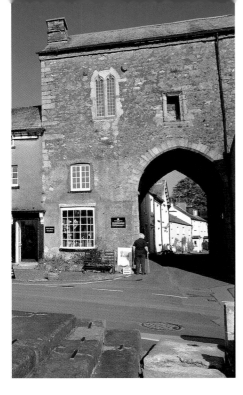

Cartmel Priory and Gatehouse

MONUMENTS

Lakeland has loads of good archaeological sites, but for many of them you'd need a magnifying glass and a portable archaeologist. But there are some where you can actually see something. The walls of *Hardknott Roman Fort* still stand, though not very high, near the top of the pass, on the left as you go up from Eskdale. You can easily miss it from the road. There's not a lot to see, compared with Hadrian's Wall, but it's still a dramatic site guarding the road from Galava to Glannaventa (Ravenglass). The Roman name was Mediobogdum. The parade ground is fascinating and the views fantastic. It's worth investigating and gives a wonderful idea of why the Romans came to a grinding halt in these far-flung places.

Hardknott Fort: or what's left of it

Castlerigg Stone Circle just off the A66, before you get into Keswick from the south, is also in a fantastic setting, surrounded by high fells, though the stones themselves are not very impressive; 38 of them in a circle, roughly 90 feet across and about 3 to 4,000 years old. Like the economy, no one can explain it.

Castlerigg Stone Circle: inexplicable

Another stone circle, *Long Meg and her Daughters*, near Little Salkeld just north of Penrith, is huge – nearly 300 feet wide. Long Meg is the tallest of 68 or so stones, about 9 feet high and covered with mysterious symbols. The 'daughters' are the other stones and the circle probably dates from around 1,500 BC. Off the beaten track, but very moody.

One of Lakeland's most famous features is the *Bowder Stone* – a large, isolated rock, apparently in a state of delicate balance (30 feet high, 60 long and about 1,900 tons of it). It stands away from the rock face, overlooking the Borrowdale valley. How it got there, no one knows. A ladder allows you to climb to the top.

The Bowder Stone

Long Meg: with some of her daughters

HUNTER'S BEST BUILDINGS

1 *Dalemain*, opposite. Not necessarily the best overall, but the best and finest stately home in North Lakeland.

2 *Levens Hall*, right. The best stately home in the Southern Lakes. Oh, let's call it joint best overall with Dalemain, so they don't fall out.

3 *Conishead Priory*, below. Can't compete with the big boys for grandeur or contents, as the Buddhists haven't got much money, but so interesting, so unexpected.

THE BEST OF LAKELAND

MOUNTAINS

Scafell: spot the Pike, then climb it, England's highest

There are four mountains in the Lake District over 3,000 feet, or three if you count Scafell Pike and Scafell as one, which they're not, as they have separate summits, but most visitors and many natives refer to having climbed 'Scafell' and mean in fact they've climbed Scafell Pike, ignoring or forgetting the twin peak of Scafell which is assumed to be part of the same, but is fifty feet lower.

Such a pity about metres. There was something satisfying and rather grand and important about getting above the magical 3,000-foot mark. Getting above 920 metres not only seems lower but not nearly as impressive. However, if only to give the printers more work, we will use both measurements in our Mountains chapter.

The four big ones are: Scafell Pike at 3,210 feet/978 metres; Scafell at 3,162 feet/964 metres; Helvellyn at 3,118 feet/950 metres; Skiddaw at 3,053 feet/931 metres.

Scafell Pike, Helvellyn and Skiddaw also happen to be the most popular mountains, climbed the most often, though figures are naturally non-existent. They haven't quite yet got to a turnstile on the top, though on busy days it could ease congestion as there is very often a queue to stand on the final cairn.

Scafell Pike (3,210 feet/978m) is England's highest and the hardest to get to of all the popular Lake District mountains – the one which has seen terrible accidents, but the one which you can boast most about, if you honestly get to the top. It's not really very difficult, but a long slow climb which means the weather is more likely to be different on top, usually worse; so be well prepared with stout footwear, some extra warmth and good rainwear.

It is part of a range of peaks known as the Scafell Pikes which you have to work your way over or round before you finally start climbing the big one, hence the relatively long time needed to get up, compared with some other mountains which happen to be much nearer civilisation or parking. That's what makes Scafell all the more special. Samuel Taylor Coleridge did it in 1802, all on his own, without a guide or companion, carrying a pen and a bottle of ink with him. He wrote a letter on top, so his is the first *recorded* climb of Scafell, then he hurried down any old way, ignoring all the easy paths, which is not to be recommended.

A ravine called Piers Gill is about the most dangerous part. In 1921, someone fell down it, breaking both ankles, and lay at the bottom for eighteen days. He was finally found, having landed near a pool of water, which had kept him alive.

The shortest and quickest but steepest route is from Wasdale Head, going up Lingmell Gill, but you have to get round and into Wasdale in the first place, which is a long drive for anyone in Central Lakeland.

It's easiest from Seathwaite, walking straight up the valley till you hit Stockley Bridge, then cut right up Sty Head Gill for Sty Head Tarn. You'll probably see hordes of walkers by the tarn, socks and boots off, resting or guzzling. Once over Sty Head Pass, you hit a long, open walk which takes you along the western flank of Scafell Pike, a route known as the Guides' Walk or the Corridor. It finally takes you straight up to the summit, over rougher, rockier ground, but still not too difficult.

The actual summit is not very exciting or pretty, being rather bleak and barren. But on a clear day the views are sensational.

On the way back, if the day is clear and you feel confident, try varying the route into Borrowdale by coming down via Sprinkling Tarn. The round trip should take about six hours. On a hot day, celebrate with a dip in the ice green, marvellous marble water at Stockley Bridge.

There are clever folks, the real climbing types, who are rather scornful about *Skiddaw* (3,053 feet/931m), dismissing it as easy peasy, nowt more than a stroll, with no hairy or horrible bits where real men can break their legs. It is rather a cuddly, rounded, modest sort of mountain, but it makes an excellent mountain walk all the same.

Skiddaw was the first popular mountain climb in Lakeland and that lovely open path from the Keswick side has been used by millions for over 150 years. You could probably take a pram up it. In the last war, motorbikes and army vehicles went up it. No bother.

In 1815, Wordsworth and Southey took their respective families for

Opposite: Skiddaw – always popular

a bonfire party to celebrate Waterloo, with the servants carrying up roast beef and plum pudding. It's that sort of friendly, accessible mountain. Terribly handy for parking.

Skiddaw dominates the Northern Fells, Big Brother over its surrounding mountain mass, a landmark for miles around, and people who live beyond it describe themselves as living Back O' Skiddaw.

You can approach it from the rear, the eastern side, which is hidden from Keswick. It's an excellent approach, hardly used, though it means a long, but exciting walk from Dash Falls. If you do this route, look out for Skiddaw House, an amazing building, stuck literally in the middle of nowhere, once used by shepherds, and now recently converted into a youth hostel and providing good shelter in bad weather.

The best-known route up Skiddaw is from Keswick. By far the most popular and probably the most dramatic, as you rise very quickly and can get good views over your shoulder, looking over Keswick and Derwentwater, and pat yourself on the back for doing so well.

Come out of Keswick and turn right just past the big roundabout, following the sign saying Skiddaw, heading up the little road towards Underscar. You eventually hit a rather rough road, Gale Road. Go right along it to the very end and you'll find car parking space probably already full, so come back and find some space on the road. This drive is a bit of a cheat, as you've saved almost 1,000 feet already. Real climbers start from Keswick and climb Latrigg first. But it means that you can come straight out of the car and can start climbing. You actually see children *running* to get up. That beautiful grassy slope, right in front of you, looks so attractive and tantalising almost like a grass ski slope. This takes you up Jenkin Hill, the first slope of Skiddaw, and it is in fact the steepest. After that, it's a long but easier walk to the summit. The top can be freezing, so take warm clothes.

Helvellyn (3,118 feet/950m) is often considered the finest mountain by Lakeland experts, for its brilliant views and exciting summit. In some ways the most dangerous – at least it seems to have more accidents than any other Lakeland mountain. But Wordsworth climbed it safely aged seventy. Makes you sick.

The best route is from Glenridding car park. Follow the lane on the other side of the beck until you reach a fork in the path. Take the left fork indicating Lanty Tarn. Follow the zigzag path to Lanty Tarn, which is set amidst trees and is very pretty. Go down the hill, through a small plantation and up onto the ridge taking the right hand path up the fellside. Grisedale valley is on your left. Once on the ridge cross over the stile and take the left hand path onto Striding Edge. The edge is narrow and involves a bit of scrambling but this can be avoided by using the path a little lower down (approx. 20 feet). Red Tarn is on the right. It gets its name because when the sun rises the tarn appears dark red in colour. It's traditional to watch the sunrise from the summit on Midsummer's Day – always a lot of people there, but worth the trip.

Getting off the Edge and onto Helvellyn is interesting (more scrambling) and the path up Helvellyn is steep. Once on the summit you can rest on the seats in the shelter and enjoy fantastic all-round views. But only experienced walkers should take this route.

Near the summit is a small monument commemorating the landing of an aeroplane on the top of Helvellyn in 1926. The two pilots from

Left: Great Gable
Below: Striding Edge, Helvellyn

Right: Bowfell and Crinkle Craggs
Below: St Johns in the Vale and
Blencathra

THE BEST OF LAKELAND

Lancashire got out, looked around, realising they needed proof of their daft caper, and decided to ask the first person approaching to take their photograph. He turned out to be a professor from Birmingham University. He took their snap and they then got back in their plane, taxied down a slope and, with a bit of a struggle, just in time, before going over the edge, they got airborn. Ah, they don't make idiots, I mean heroes, like that any more.

Other big or biggish mountains worth attempting include:

Bow Fell (2,960 feet/902m) On a clear day you can see as far as Ingleborough in the Pennines and even Snaefell on the Isle of Man.

Great Gable (2,949 feet/899m) You get good views into Wasdale Valley and of the Scafells.

Pillar (2,927 feet/892m) Most routes are very steep and only for the sure footed.

Coniston Old Man

Blencathra (2,847 feet/868m) Or Saddleback, as it's also known. Adventurous walkers can follow the footpath along Sharp Edge – the best ridge walk in the Lake District (best not to undertake this route in the wet).

Crinkle Crags (2,816 feet/858m) The quickest and easiest route onto Crinkle Crags is from the Three Shire Stone at the top of Wrynose Pass, going over Cold Pike.

High Street (2,718 feet/829m) The cairn on Thornthwaite Crag is about 14 feet high, which must be one of the most remarkable in the Lake District – only a short distance from the summit of High Street.

Coniston Old Man (2,635 feet/803m) A much loved, much climbed old gent, who has been left with some nasty facial scars over the centuries, thanks to the mining, but still welcomes careful climbers.

FELLS

Fells are mountains which didn't grow, but they can provide just as much pleasure, and even danger, as their big brothers. There are several around 1,000 to 2,000 feet high which are recommended:

Castle Crag (980 feet/299m) A small crag with old slate quarries, north of Rosthwaite, Borrowdale. There are marvellous views all round – it's probably one of the best viewpoints in the Borrowdale area.

Cat Bells (1,481 feet/451m) Very good views in all directions, especially into Newlands Valley and there's a very attractive walk beside the lakeshore. Good fun for a family outing.

Harter Fell (2,129 feet/649m) In the Dunnerdale Valley. The summit is quite craggy and provides a good playground for children. Good views to the Scafells and Dow Crag range.

Haystacks (1,959 feet/597m) On the south-west side of Buttermere. Easiest approach is from Honister, or you can go up gently from Gatesgarth, Buttermere.

Helm Crag (1,299 feet/396m) North of Grasmere village. Can be combined with Easdale Tarn and Sour Milk Ghyll, just to vary the scenery.

Loughrigg Fell (1,101 feet/336m) Good views over Grasmere and area. The real summit is the one with the trig point. Spectacular views.

Walla Crag, Borrowdale (1,234 feet/376m) Above the B5289 south of Keswick, the first craggy outcrop high on the left as you drive down the valley.

Left: Helm Crag
Below: Castle Crag, left, and
Loughrigg Fell

HUNTER'S TOP
MOUNTAINS AND FELLS

How can you compare them? The answer is you can't, but looking into my portfolio of climbs and bank of memories, and if forced to take only three hills, which I have to climb for ever in some walking paradise, then I'll want a selection, a variety of big and small, easy and peasy, all of which have wonderful, personal associations for me.

1 *Skiddaw*. High enough, as mountains go, but not hard, which is one of its attractions. Easy to get to as well. It's the one I've climbed most often. I love the idea of Wordsworth and chums climbing it to celebrate Waterloo. My wife and children climbed it in the dark to celebrate Prince Charles's wedding (his first one). I stayed in the car that evening, with a poorly knee, but I was with them in spirit.

2 *Haystacks*. It's the Wainwright associations which does it. This is where he wanted his ashes to be scattered so I'll always think of him there, as will every other Wainwright lover.

3 *Cat Bells*. The ultimate family walk, it just goes up and up, very gently, leading you on as if for ever, the first introduction to Lakeland fells for thousands of children over the centuries, where I took my own, when they were young.

Cat Bells: ultimate family walk

Left: Skiddaw – for best of all mountain climbs

Below: Haystacks for Wainwright's ashes

THE BEST OF LAKELAND

Ullswater: frozen assets, held safe for us all

With age and my dodgy knees, I don't expect to be doing many high mountains in the future, alas, but the thrill of racing to the top, or more usually struggling to the final cairn, and experiencing that sudden surge of satisfaction and completion, I'll always remember that, and be grateful. I still have the images of most of those views from the tops lodged in my mind.

In Lakeland, there are as many walks as there are walkers. You can sit down in advance and create your own from the map, or make it up as you go along, chop and change, short cut and long cut, divert or convert.

These days, I like a walk to be round. I don't like dragging straight up, that's for fell runners, only to come straight down again the same way. A sort of circle is best, slowly up a valley, through a gap, easily on to the top, then round the other side, preferably near a lake, back to base, without repeating one step. I don't like it too steep, especially coming down. Hurts the old knees. I like variety, smooth bits and rough bits. I don't want any roads, but I do like paths I can find easily, especially those grassy swards which look as if the Great Gardener in the sky had got out his celestial lawnmower to the side of the fell. I definitely want views, especially containing a lake, and I want to feel impressed by myself, look how far we've got, haven't we done well. I like a top that is a top, with a cairn we can crouch beside, scoffing the while. And back at the beginning, I like the thought of a pub or hotel nearby, for emergencies, such as more scoff. My wife hates screes, so we are not allowed anywhere near them, certainly not. On family walks, the children have their own requirement – it must be a new walk, one we haven't done before. Oh the hours I have studied the OS and old Wainwright, getting further and further afield, trying to work out new routes which will keep us all happy. Many of those books of family walks you see are full of the obvious stuff, often lifted from each other, which any idiot can work out for themselves, such as walking to Friar's Crag. I don't want them as easy as that. I like a walk which can spread itself across the day, with two hours up, a picnic and lots of rests, then two hours to stroll back. The joy when we find a new one, which we like to think we have created, carving it out of the contours, shaping it in our minds. And after all these years, we can still manage to find them.

But looking back, thinking hard, there are three walks I hope to do over and over again, as long as the knees will last.

Ullswater. Our all-time favourite walking area is around the far shore of Ullswater, that section where there's no road. Everything is there, all the sights and sensations, and all in a fairly short space. There are two ways of doing it, either by driving round the lake to Howtown, then doing a round walk, ending back at your car; or by taking the steamer there and back across the lake. Either way, you are in for sheer pleasure.

Park at the little church of Martindale, above Howtown, just on the top after the switchback road, then walk down the little twisting road and into Bore Dale. It starts off like easy Beatrix Potter country, all smooth and rounded, but as you proceed up the valley, the fields and farmhouses run out and it gets wilder and emptier. Climb up to the head of the valley, through the Hause or pass. The path is clear and the walking easy, though it gets a little steep towards the end. Once over the top, bear right, heading down towards Patterdale. Admire the views, then pick up the path which leads along the shore of Ullswater, underneath the flanks of Place Fell. The path twists and turns with the shape of the lake, giving a different but equally wonderful view at every angle. At Sandwick, you can carry on, if you're not tired, and take in the walk round Hallin Fell, or turn right up the little road, back up the hill to the car. About 10 miles in all. The perfect walk. Allow four hours.

The other way is to leave the car at Glenridding and catch the steamer to Howtown. On leaving the pier, turn right through several gates and go onto the fellside track above Waternook. Continue along the footpath, descending to the water's edge before entering woodland below Hallin Fell. Cross the little road at Sandwick and walk up towards Townhead Cottage, where you should turn right and follow the wall before crossing Scalehow Beck. Descend to Long Crag and the lake shore. The next mile is through attractive open and wooded slopes. Below Silver Crag, the bridleway divides. Keep to the path nearest the lake and follow it back to Patterdale, then follow the road to Glenridding.

Buttermere. From Buttermere village car park, follow the path to the left of the Fish Hotel. Take the left-hand path through the kissing gate, cross the footbridge and follow the left-hand path around the lake's southern shore. At the head of the lake, go left across the fields and rejoin the road. As the road runs alongside the lake, watch out for a small car park on your left. Leave the road here and follow the shoreline once more, back towards the village.

A pretty walk. Perfectly round, perfectly pleasing.

Derwentwater. You can walk the whole of the lake, but you'll end up on some road bits. Best to use the boats, then you can hop off or on, expanding or shortening the distance. An easy three mile walk is to take the launch from Friar's Crag and get off at Hawse End. Follow the lakeshore footpath left (it goes through a field for a short while, leaving the shore). Keep to the path at the edge of the lake until it reaches the Brandlehow landing stage, then bear right until you reach a fork. Go left up some steps, through the kissing gate and then keep left between the cottage and boathouse. At the next fork in the path, go right across some rather boggy ground then join another path going left to the shore. Follow the footpath until it joins the road, then go left to the Lodore landing stage, where you can catch a launch back to Friar's Crag.

There are some good views on the walk, both of surrounding fells and of the islands, particularly St Herbert's. Watch out for the Floating Island at Lodore – you might be lucky.

Buttermere. Pretty perfect

You might have noticed that all three of my best walks involve lakes. And are also pretty handy for me to get to from Loweswater. I want ease of access and ease of pleasure these days, not a long, hard grind.

But the point of going round a lake, or ending up along a lake, is that Lakes are what we are, what makes us so special. Other parts of the globe have lots of hills and mountains, but rarely do they have so many stretches of water, so handily placed, so prettily displayed. Lakes do set off the scenery so nicely, surrounded or framed by hills

and fells, perfect pictures for the eye to take in and retain for ever.

Even if you have been doing a high walk, or a hairy climb, you eventually have to come down. I don't think the National Park people would be keen for you to stay up there, not for ever. Think of the planning problems. We all have to come down to ground level and, with a bit of luck, we will arrive at a lake, take a final stroll along the shore, a last look at the evening boats, and from there, look back and up to where we have been. Ah, the perfect end to a perfect Lakeland day.

Derwentwater: drawing to a close, another day, another scene, then the final chapter is over...

PHOTOGRAPHIC ACKNOWLEDGEMENTS

David Addison, Senhouse Roman Museum 80

The Armitt Trust 87, 93, 94 (top), 98

David Bailey 49 (top)

E. A. Bowness 38 (top), 135 (bottom right)

Dorothy Burrows 29, 35, 60 (right), 61 (top), 62 (top), 64, 67 (bottom right) 69, 75, 77 (bottom), 85 (bottom), 88, 90, 91, 102, 104, 108, 112, 123

Cars of the Stars 81

Dave Coates 42

Val Corbett 12, 30 (top), 46 (bottom), 67 (bottom left)

Alan Curtis 37, 53, 57, 99

Julie Fryer 40 (bottom), 47 (top), 54, 66, 70 (top), 97, 100, 101, 113, 115, 133, 135 (top), 137 (bottom)

James Guilliam 40 (top), 114

Fred Hill 9, 30 (bottom), 44, 45, 46 (top), 50, 55, 60 (left), 65, 67 (top right), 68, 82, 92, 109 (top), 119 (top), 120, 122, 124, 129, 136

David W. Jones 62 (bottom), 63, 67 (top left), 70 (bottom), 72, 86, 107, 109 (bottom left)

Lakeland Arts Trust 79, 85 (top and middle)

Lakeland Motor Museum, Holker Hall and Gardens 77 (top)

Manjushri Mahayana Buddhist Centre 125 (bottom)

Miller Howe Restaurant 17

Rod Moore, Cumberland Toy and Model Museum 74

The Sharrow Bay Hotel 16

Ivor Nicholas 109 (bottom right)

Tom Parker 6, 15, 18, 21, 31, 36, 38 (bottom), 94 (bottom), 110, 135 (bottom left), 131

Kenneth L. Price 118

Alan Robinson 61 (bottom)

Jill Swainson 117, 125 (top)

David Tarn 2, 10-11, 14, 24, 27, 33, 34, 41, 43, 47 (bottom), 48, 49 (bottom), 71, 121, 132 (bottom), 137 (top), 138, 141, 142-3

Phil Woolley 116, 119 (bottom), 126, 132 (top)